Screenplays as I Dramas 10

ALLEGED

**An Historical Drama Movie Script
About the Scopes Monkey Trial**

Screenplay
by
Brian James Godawa
And
Frederick C. Foote

Alleged: An Historical Drama Movie Script About the Scopes Monkey Trial
Screenplays as Literature Series • Dramas • 10
1st Edition

Copyright © 2019 Brian James Godawa
All rights reserved. No part of this script book may be reproduced in any form or by any electronic or mechanical means, including information storage and retrieval systems, without prior written permission, except in the case of brief quotations in critical articles and reviews.

Cover images used under license from Frederick C. Foote.

Warrior Poet Publishing
www.warriorpoetpublishing.com

ISBN: 978-1-942858-70-6 (paperback)
ISBN: 978-1-942858-71-3 (ebook)

Get this FREE Ebooklet

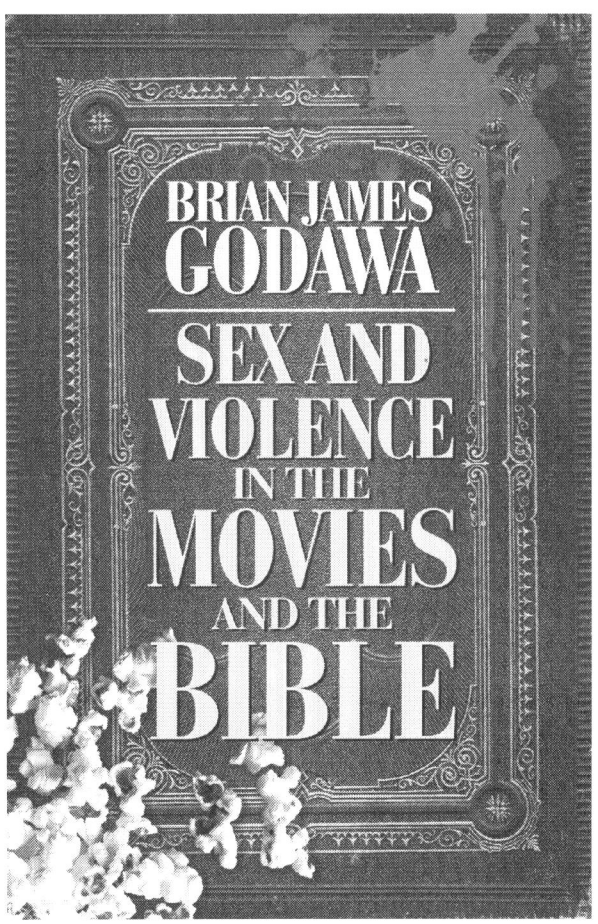

Too Much Sex and Violence in the Movies?

That's what some Christians argue. But just how much is enough? Author Brian Godawa examines the Bible to see how it depicts the sins of humanity accurately without exploitation.

Just click on this link to get your FREE ebooklet:

https://godawa.com/sex-and-violence-ebook/

Table of Contents

Title Page i
Get this FREE Ebooklet iii
Table of Contents iv
How to Read a Screenplay v
   Why This Series? vi
   Understanding the Format vii
   Scene Headings viii
   Action viii
   Dialogue x
Introduction to Alleged Screenplay xii
"ALLEGED" 1
More Screenplays as Literature 136
Sign Up to Get Brian Godawa's Updates, Movie Reviews, Other Scripts & Books. 137
Get 25% OFF the Informative Hollywood Worldviews Online Course 138
Book Series by Brian Godawa 139
About the Author 140

How to Read a Screenplay

The essential purpose of a screenplay is to be a blueprint out of which a movie is made. For this reason, screenplays or scripts are technically unfinished "works in progress." Movies are ultimately complex productions that are built from that blueprint that not only add the visual and audible aspects, but involve dozens of other creative artists' input, from the director to the actors to the costume designers, set designers and more. It has been said that there are three movies: the movie that is written in the script, the movie that is shot and the movie that is edited. That is because each step of that process involves creative input and changes that shape the movie into its final form. That final form is sometimes a faithful adaptation of the original screenplay, and sometimes a very different creature altogether.

Many movies are adapted from books or other sources, but when it comes to "spec scripts" or scripts written on speculation by a writer (with the hope that he can sell it after it is written), it all begins with the script. As the mighty Steven Spielberg once said, "If it ain't on the page, it ain't on the stage." It is the script that launches the ship and it is the script that draws and even guides the producers, the director, the actors and many others like a blueprint for a building that draws contractors, carpenters, electricians and more to construct the final edifice.

A spec script is the first embodiment of the story that grabs the hearts and imaginations of its readers and inspires them to get the resources together to make it into a movie. The power of that blueprint is its ability to convey an entertaining story. In Hollywood, as in most of life, story is king.

But because a screenplay is a blueprint, it is a kind of unfinished "outline" for a movie. It does not convey many details like a novel can. For instance, a script gives brief descriptions of characters and only passing references to locations where events take place. Casting, costuming, set design as well as music and other elements will all be added to the movie by other professionals who expand that original story into a multilayered existential work of art.

Apart from the use of some narration, a movie script does not delve much into the inner mental thoughts of characters. It is more external than a novel. More visual and active, because the final movie form will be visual and active. That is, the reader must infer what is going on inside the characters based on their behavior, choices and words.

Also, a screenplay must cover story ground in less time than other mediums like novels. For example, good dialogue is usually shorter, more economical, it communicates more in fewer words, driven in part by the fact that a movie is about one-and-a-half to two hours long which translates to roughly 120 pages in a script (1 page per minute of final screen time). And as you will see, those pages are not full of text like a book is. Everything is shorter, briefer, more concise, similar to how short stories are compared to novels.

In this sense, a screenplay reader must be more sophisticated and attentive in their reading. Every scene, every gesture, every visual reference, every word must have a purpose in a screenplay. And all of it ideally integrates into the meaning that the storyteller is conveying. Now, there are exceptions to all these things, but my main concern is to help prepare the reader of this series to read a bit differently than usual.

Because of this abbreviated "external" approach to storytelling, reading a script requires active engagement on the part of the reader, who must sometimes decipher meanings, symbols, and character motivations like a detective. But the effort is well worth it as the reader becomes more skilled at watching movies and television with greater appreciation.

So, the strength of a movie script is that it is the essence of the story, its heart and soul, the primal foundation upon which a movie is built and expanded. That is why I am publishing the Screenplays as Literature Series, because despite the format being an abbreviated starting point, it is still a powerful way to tell a great story, indeed, to visualize a movie before it is made.

Reading a screenplay can be like watching a movie in your mind.

Why This Series?

Most of the screenplays in the Screenplays as Literature Series are unproduced. That means they have not been sold or made into movies. One might therefore conclude that they are not very good stories if they could not garner the interest of producers to buy them.

I will let the reader be the final arbiter of that decision. But let me at least make the argument that it is also equally possible that there are plenty of other reasons why these screenplays could be very good stories and yet still not produced.

Everyone in Hollywood knows that there are too many excellent scripts that don't get made. Sometimes it's because they don't recognize truly unique genius (the secret desire of every writer). With the studio blockbuster mentality, many producers and studios are looking for "more of the same" to make big money fast: prequels, sequels, rip-offs and spin-offs. Many great movies, like Schindler's List and Forrest Gump, had a history of being rejected by every major studio in town and taking as long as ten or more years to get made—by the biggest producers in town!

In Hollywood there are a million bad reasons why good scripts don't get sold or made. It could be political incorrectness or other "social justice" censorship, it could be budget, it could be scheduling conflicts, it could be sea changes at studios, it could be creative differences or infighting. Often, it's the worst reason in the world, and the most common: You don't know the right people at the right time.

It's actually a miracle that any movie gets made. So, a lot of good ones languish unread or unproduced on the shelves of writers and others who just couldn't get people to see their scripts were undiscovered Oscar winners. I say that, not sarcastically, but with full sincerity. I believe it. Although, I would have to walk back the "Oscar" praise, since the Academy Awards have increasingly become less a sign of recognized excellence and more a sign of inbred political incest.

There is something called "The Blacklist" every year that is a list of recent scripts in Hollywood that are considered excellent by many readers, that have made the rounds, that everyone "in the know" has read, that are excellent, but yet never get made for a multitude of these very reasons listed above.

So, the point is that "unproduced" does not necessarily mean "bad." Sadly, that means that both the genius and the self-deluded amateur are in the same boat. Neither of them knows if their rejected script is an undiscovered masterpiece or a rejected delusion of mediocrity.

Am I an undiscovered Mozart or am I simply Salieri?

Again, I will let you the reader decide when it comes to the scripts in this series.

I just hope you enjoy these stories as much as I enjoyed writing them.

Understanding the Format

I will describe how to understand some of the unique formatting of a screenplay to help avoid confusion for the reader not acquainted with script formatting.

My first and foremost advice is to try to picture yourself watching a movie as you read the text. This is, after all, a script for a movie. So why not read it that way? You will have to imagine a lot of details to fill in the gaps of what costume designers, make-up artists, set designers and others would normally bring to the production of the script. But some readers actually like doing that.

Maybe a character may remind you of your favorite actor. So, imagine that actor as you read their action and dialogue. But notice every detail, every nuance of dialogue, because, as I noted earlier, every single detail is there for a reason.

Though I have formatted these screenplays basically as they were written, I have made some changes to make it easier for readers who are not in the film business. Normally, screenplays are written in courier font. Courier is an ugly font, so in the print version of this script I changed it to a more legible one that most readers will be comfortable with. I want to make it easier for you, not harder.

If you are reading this in ebook format, you can alter the font and spacing to whatever format you want to read it in.

But let's get going with our quick lesson on how to read a script.

Scene Headings

After reading, "FADE IN," the reader will first notice what is called a "Scene Heading." It looks something like this:

INT. DUNGEON CORRIDOR - NIGHT

This is the notation of the location where the next scene is taking place. It helps the moviemakers organize for their shooting, but for the reader, it tells us quickly where the scene takes place.

The first element will either be "**INT**." which stands for interior, or "**EXT**." which stands for exterior. So, we know if we are inside a location or outside.

The next element of the scene heading is the actual location, such as "**DUNGEON CORRIDOR**." It is the briefest way of referring to that location. If there is some description in the paragraph below it, it will be very sparse, like painting a quick emotional picture of the feel of where we are, as opposed to wordy detailed descriptions. So, you will have to conjure up in your own mind what it looks like, like the set designer and costume designer does later. Hey, you'll be like a movie director!

Then we have "**NIGHT**" or "**DAY**." These are also quick designations for the shooting schedule, but they also tell us as readers what part of a day we are in.

Sometimes, the scene headings are shortened. If you already established "EXT... DAY" and then follow the character walking into the house, you need to alert the reader that he is now in "INT," but you don't have to necessarily add "DAY" again, because it was a continuous movement. So be prepared for some shortened scene headings to make the reading flow smoother.

Action

Usually below that scene heading is what is called the "action." Here is what it looks like with a scene heading before it:

INT. DUNGEON CORRIDOR - NIGHT

TWO CLOAKED FIGURES slither through the shadows of a medieval dungeon corridor. SCREAMS of torture. Rats SQUEAL.

Action describes any actions of characters we will see. Again, it is sparse and to the point and focused on what we are going to see on the screen, not what is in the character's head. Every word counts.

And because of that economy of language, do not expect grammar that follows the Chicago Manual of Style. Sentence fragments often rule the day because they keep the pace moving, like you are watching a movie, rather than reading a novel.

Sometimes a writer may add a stylistic flourish and tell us what the reader should conclude based on what we are seeing. So, you might see something like, "He obviously doesn't want to go with her." This is internal and might only be conveyed in the facial gesture of the actor. But since we cannot see the actors in the script, writers must sometimes cheat to help the reader understand what the viewer of the movie will be more capable of seeing.

You will notice the ALL CAPS words. Usually, when a character shows up for the first time anywhere in the script, their names are in all caps. It is a way of easily finding them for the movie makers, but it also helps the reader realize a new presence in the story.

Also, as in the example above, special effects, such as sounds or visual effects, are also capitalized to bring notice to the filmmakers for their production purposes. For the reader, this alerts us to the importance of a sound or image that would be more obvious to a movie viewer than a script reader.

This goes for underlined words as well. Underlining is like focusing the camera on something.

Sometimes, the scene headings and action can be used in a simpler format to differentiate complex action or visuals within a single location. You want it to read easily and quickly so you get a sense of the pace of the scene and aren't slowed down by details. Here is an example:

SLOW MOTION SHOT

Dragut's warhorse breaks through the cloud of smoke and fighting. He sees La Valette against a flagpole.

STARKEY AND THE MONSTER

Back up against the wall. A whack by the Monster snaps one of Starkey's swords in two.

LA VALETTE AND DRAGUT

battle around the flagpole. With a CLANG, their blades cross against the pole and freeze, straining against each other.

In this example, we are in one location, and two fights are going on that would be easily edited visually to follow for the audience. But for the reader, I tell them that first, they see a SLOW MOTION SHOT of the bad guy Dragut arriving. Then we jump over to a battle between the two characters STARKEY AND THE MONSTER, and then a jump back to Dragut who is now fighting the character LaValette.

Sometimes you might see something like this:

SUPER: ISTANBUL, TURKEY

This is called a "super" and it is short for "superimposed." It's basically like those titles we see at the bottom of the screen when we are introduced to a new location or to some introductory material like that famous screen-crawl at the beginning of each Star Wars movie.

Dialogue

When characters speak in a script, this is what it looks like:

                GUARD
        Ho. Where does ye think yer goin'?
            (beat)
        Ya looks shady to me.

The character's name is in all caps, so we clearly know who is speaking from what is being said. Before a character speaks, they must be described as present in the action first. Otherwise, they are popping in like a quantum fluctuation, which would be confusing to us Newtonian readers :-).

But also notice the word "beat" in parentheses. These are called, quite helpfully, "parentheticals," and they are used for several purposes. The word "beat" above, simply means a meaningful pause. It will affect the context of the words spoken or indicates a change of direction in dialogue. You can imagine the character pausing before they say their next lines, which adds nuance to the dialogue.

You might also read parentheticals with descriptions like "sarcastic," or "angrily," or something similar.

>   JANE
>   (sarcastic)
>   Don't you look pretty.

This is done when the words themselves may not obviously communicate to the reader what a viewer can see on the screen. "Don't you look pretty" could be either genuine or sarcastic and you might not be able to determine that unless you saw the actress saying it with her facial gestures. So, the writer cheats a bit to help us catch what we cannot see.

You might also read an action in the parenthetical like "(To the other guy)" or "(he looks closer)." These would be used to describe actions done in the middle of talking, such as changing the character to whom they are talking.

Sometimes, you might see the unique parentheticals, (O.S.) and (V.O.) after the character name rather than below it:

>   JOHN (O.S.)
>   Put that gun down.

>   JANE (V.O.)
>   I realized John was not everything he said he was.

(O.S.) means "off-screen." It means that we hear the voice of the character, but we do not see them as we are watching the "movie in our minds." They are outside the camera view, but still in the scene.

(V.O.) means "voice-over," and is used when the character's voice is a narrator that is not within the actual story but is commenting upon it from outside the story. It's narration.

Well, there it is, your quick lesson on script-reading. It's not much different than reading plays. If you know the basic elements, it becomes quite easy to watch the movie in your mind as you read the script!

Introduction to Alleged Screenplay

The image that most people have in their minds of the infamous Scopes Monkey Trial was that of a bunch of uneducated small town fundamentalist yokels in 1925 attacking evolution taught in public schools; and that of Bible thumping sweaty religious fanatic William Jennings Bryan being destroyed on the stand by the brilliant erudite atheist lawyer Clarence Darrow.

The source that is almost single-handedly responsible for this image is the old black and white movie *Inherit the Wind*, starring Spencer Tracy as the Darrow character and Frederick March as the Bryan character.

And this image is almost completely a lie.

Well, we all know the best lies have a little bit of truth in them, but the movie cleverly made a "fictionalized" version of the story with different names of the real life characters. This was so they could avoid being accused of the slander and lies they presented in the movie.

The real story was how the media and educational elite manipulated and spun the truth into a lie in order to take control of the reins of information power. Sound familiar? Sound like today?

When Fred Foote asked me to write the screenplay with him for a movie based on the scholarly book *Summer of the Gods*, I jumped at the opportunity. The goal was to tell a fair and truthful version of that infamous story, like fact-checking fake news.

We chose to do that by telling the true story through the eyes of a fictional hero, young journalist wannabe Charles Anderson. So, yes, we use some fiction as creative license, but the major facts of the story are accurate, in fact, a lot of it was drawn from actual quotations of the famous characters involved. Speeches, written articles and other key moments are quoted in the script from William Jennings Bryan, Clarence Darrow and H.L. Mencken. The hyperbolic language of Mencken used to slander his opponents like "ombibulous, bucolic buncombe, imbeciles, yokels, forworn backwaters" and his misogyny and bigotry were taken directly from his writings. He really did speak and write with that cynical bitter edge.

Actual medical language supporting euthanasia and sterilization was drawn from magazines and legal papers of that time. And the trial was drawn from the public domain transcripts of the actual trial. Again, we use some creative license to draw together the drama of the narrative, but our goal was to bring a more accurate accounting of that historical event that showed the strengths and weaknesses of both sides.

The screenplay is rich with several themes that are amazingly relevant for today. Fake news is not a new thing. Mencken and others were guilty of it back then, through selective quoting of facts, hyperbolic adjectives, and even outright lies. The media was the enemy back then as now. And the result is the same: truth is sacrificed at the altar of power. Looking back on it now, we bring out the irony of now-known frauds like Piltdown Man and Nebraska Man being believed as gospel science. And euthanasia being considered the medical consensus opinion.

Another theme in the story is that ideas have consequences. Many people like to accuse religious believers of their ideas holding back progress, but they don't like to think through the result of their own beliefs. The screenplay brings out the very real logical consistency of Social Darwinism, the application of evolution and survival of the fittest to social engineering. The movement for sterilization and ultimately euthanasia of the mentally handicapped actually began in America. Nazi doctors in Germany drew from our own legal language reflected in evolutionary theory and the Supreme Court decision of Buck v. Bell. Justice Oliver Wendell Holmes echoed this evil support for human experimentation in his statement that "three generations of imbeciles is enough." Modern psychiatric hospitals are now known to have used some barbaric cruel treatments on the mentally handicapped, all accurately reflected in the script from historical sources.

And there is also the Nietzsche connection as well. Nazi ideology drew from Nietzsche as well as evolution. Both Darrow and Mencken were fond of Nietzsche's nihilism to bolster their own "ends justify the means" values. In the script, we deal with the Leopold and Loeb case that Darrow was involved in. Most of his statements about it were taken from the real trial. He quite accurately concluded that the two infamous murderers could not be responsible for their actions because they are simply determined by blind purposeless chance in a random universe without moral absolutes.

Well, technically, he is right. IF evolution is true, then evil is not real, it's just subjective and relative, and human choices are merely determined by nature. What else would that doctrine result in, but in murder without remorse? Again, this is still relevant for today, with our public schools indoctrinating a generation of children with anti-biblical serial killer morality.

Another dirty little secret of Darwinian evolution is its racist essence. Of course evolutionists now claim evolution does not justify the white supremacy they once thought it did, but that would simply be an absolute moral claim that is incoherent in an evolutionary worldview. The truth is that survival of the fittest in an amoral universe is justification for all acts of violence against fellow animals. The denial of this logical conclusion by evolutionists is a denial of their entire system. Another theme we bring out in the script.

In one of the foreshadowing moments of the script, an ACLU lawyer asks

Bryan, "I respect your concern for the rights of the majority. But what if one day, the tables are turned, and it's your view that is in the minority?" And that is exactly what has happened. The tables have turned, and now a belief in intelligent design by a Creator is in a worse position than mere minority in public schools. It's actually censored and those who hold to it are blacklisted. Darwinism and other forms of evolution now worship the power they wield against intellectual dissent with a fundamentalist zeal.

Consider this screenplay truth to power.

Brian James Godawa
Author and Screenwriter, *Alleged*

"ALLEGED"

Figure 1: Brian Dennehy as Clarence Darrow and Fred Thompson as William Jennings Bryan.

OPENING CREDITS

Vintage photos and reels, circa 1900-1925: Changing times. Dangerous times. New Orleans Jazz. Louis Armstrong. Lynchings. The KKK. The Stock Market. Baseball. Babe Ruth. Women's suffrage. Coal Mines. Blacks in deep poverty. World War I. German troops in gas masks. Prohibition. Al Capone. Gangsters. Flappers. The Charleston. Ford factory assembly lines. The Model T everywhere. Billy Sunday preaching. Anti-evolution crusades.

The voice of experienced activist lawyer…

> CLARENCE DARROW (V.O.)
> I sometimes wonder if I am dreaming. If in the first quarter of the twentieth century there has come back into the hearts of men the hate and feeling and the lust for blood which possesses the primitive savage of barbarous land. The human race is not a proper subject for worship. It has always taken itself too seriously. It amounts to little.
> (beat)
> I have always believed that man has little or nothing to do with himself. He is born without

willing. He dies when his time is up. He is
influenced by everything about him, helpless from
the beginning to the end.
>　(beat)

The principle thing to remember is that we have
little or no control, as individuals, over ourselves,
and that criminals are like the rest of us in that
regard. This is life and all there is of life; to play
the game, to play the cards we get; and play them
to the end. The game may not be worth the while.
The stakes may not be worth the winning. But we
should play it bravely to the end.

INT. LARGE CHICAGO CITY COURTROOM - DAY

SUPER: CHICAGO, 1924.

A courtroom packed with hundreds of people. Standing room only. The trial of the century. But you can hear a pin drop as they're all waiting for the next word to come out of the mouth of a lone man addressing the JUDGE.

CLARENCE DARROW (68). The weight of experience in his creased face. Gruff, unkempt, salty. His trademark: pastel shirt and tie, colored suspenders, a generation out of date. But when he speaks, all the world listens. He continues from the previous voice-over.

>　DARROW
> I can sum up the prosecutor's arguments in a
> minute. Cruel, dastardly, premeditated, fiendish,
> and malignant of heart.

The clean-cut PROSECUTOR gives a look of shock.

Over in the press box, writer H.L. MENCKEN (45) scrutinizes Darrow with a sly grin as the others around him write feverishly on their pads. He's got a dapper big-city suit, signature haircut: parted down the middle, Vaseline flat.

Darrow walks back over to his table, his heart bleeding.

>　DARROW
> Now, that is what I have listened to for three days
> against two minors - two children - who have no

right to even sign their names on a legal document.

Figure 2: Colin Meaney as H.L. Mencken

The TWO BOYS at the table, aged 18 and 19, peer up at Darrow like scared rabbits. Beautiful, fair. Portraits of innocence.

>DARROW
>These unfortunate lads sit here hated, despised, outcasts, with the community shouting for their blood.

The insulted crowd RUMBLES. A WOMAN crosses herself. A MOTHER behind the prosecution weeps, consoled by her husband. The JUDGE bangs his gavel.

Darrow smirks, satisfied. The whole room in his hands. His delivery is poetry.

>DARROW
>Your Honor, What we are is determined by heredity and environment. Nature is strong and she is pitiless, and we are her victims. In the words of old Omar Khayyam: we are only

> impotent pieces in the game He plays, Upon this checkerboard of nights and days, Hither and thither moves, and checks, and slays, And one by one back in the closet lays.

He finishes with the compassion of Christ himself.

> DARROW
> I am pleading for life, charity, kindness, and the infinite mercy that considers all. I am pleading that we overcome cruelty with kindness and hatred with love. Your Honor, let these boys live.

The two boys wipe tears from their eyes in the ensuing silence. As do others in the crowd. But most amazing of all, the Judge is also tearing up. Cameras flash.

EXT. LARGE CHICAGO CITY COURTHOUSE - DAY

More cameras flash on Darrow, now standing on the courthouse steps surrounded by a tight-knit group of reporters. The two defendant boys are beside him, but this is not really about them. It's about the great Clarence Darrow.

> REPORTER
> Mr. Darrow! Who do you plan to defend next?!

> DARROW
> Myself.

The crowd laughs.

> DARROW
> As of today, I am officially retiring.

The reporters sigh "Awwwwwww."

> REPORTER
> What does your wife think of you retiring?

But before Darrow can give a reply...

> MENCKEN
> What does your mistress think?

Shamefully fun "oohhs" and "aahhs" pepper the crowd.

Darrow looks over at Mencken stepping out from the crowd, a cigar proudly in his grinning mouth, cynically above it all. Darrow smiles.

> DARROW
> Well, we'll just keep that between us men, why don't we?

More laughs of approval from the crowd.

> DARROW
> That is, unless the great H.L. Mencken here wants to make me an object of his biting satire.

It's almost a challenge, almost a plea for mercy.

> MENCKEN
> And give ammunition to fundamentalist bigots? When hell freezes over.

Everyone laughs. Mencken and Darrow share a wink and a nod.

EXT. ESTABLISHING SHOTS OF DAYTON, TENNESSEE - DAY

The lush rolling green hills and farms of rural southern Tennessee provide a vast landscape of peace and contemplation.

Horses pull a wagon past a weathered sign: "DAYTON, TENNESSEE, POPULATION 3,000 1,800".

Nearby a MAN erects a sign that advertises "300 ACRES FOR SALE BY THE CUMBERLAND COAL COMPANY. CONTACT GEORGE RAPPLEYEA." A Model T passes the horse in ironic contrast.

Downtown Dayton is not much to look at in terms of architecture. But what it lacks in sophistication, it makes up for in heart and soul. It's everything that's good about small town America. A tidy, clean, quiet community.

Mothers with their children buying fruits and vegetables at outdoor markets.

Farmers picking up tools from the hardware store. Laughing, enjoying life.

Model Ts on the streets prove they're no strangers to progress.

The local Barbershop, with its afternoon old-timers chewing the fat over newspapers.

A few doors down is the small local Newspaper office, with its proudly crafted typographic sign: "THE DAYTON HERALD."

INT. DAYTON HERALD NEWSPAPER OFFICE - DAY

CHARLES ANDERSON (23) is intertwined with an old pamphlet press, trying to fix it. He reaches for a screw deep in the guts of the machinery, grease smears on his face.

ROSE WILLIAMS (22) approaches with a couple plates of sandwiches. She's a natural beauty, untainted innocence.

Figure 3: Ashley Johnson as Rose and Nathan West as Charles.

> ROSE
> Charles. Lunch.

Charles pulls himself out of the press. Wipes his hands on a rag. Picks up a newspaper he had been reading. He's a hungry young lion with stars in his eyes. He holds up a copy of the Baltimore Sun with the headline, "LEOPOLD AND LOEB TO LIVE." Below it, a picture of Darrow and the two boys.

> CHARLES
> This is where it's at, Rose. The big cities, big papers -- big stories.

> ROSE
> Big murders.

Charles pokes the by-line of the story: "BY H.L. MENCKEN."

                    CHARLES
          The greatest journalist in America -- H.L.
          Mencken.

                    ROSE
          Could the great H.L. Mencken single-handedly
          buy and repair a pamphlet press?

                    CHARLES
                 (not as impressed)
          For seed catalogs?

                    ROSE
          Charles. It was a great idea to bring in some more
          money to the newspaper. And it was your idea.

But Charles is still lost in the Baltimore Sun paper.

                    CHARLES
          My dad used to talk about him all the time.

He looks up at her with affection.

                    CHARLES
          Rose, how'd you like to live in Baltimore?

                    ROSE
                 (coy)
          Just what are you asking me, Charles Anderson?

Charles looks in her eyes. But before he can gather the courage--

They're interrupted by MR. LeBARRON (70), old-school newspaperman, but with a soul, followed by a couple INTERNS. He's carrying a simple cake with a fizzing sparkler on it.

                    LEBARRON AND INTERNS
          For he's a jolly good fellow!
          For he's a jolly good fellow!
          For he's a jolly good fellow!
          Which nobody can deny!

LeBarron bumps into the press. It's a bit clunky and in the way. Rose smiles. Charles closes his eyes in embarrassment.

> MR. LEBARRON
> Now, Charles. First place in a statewide journalist competition is nothin' to sneeze at.
>
> ROSE
> Your father would be proud.
>
> CHARLES
> (ignoring that)
> Too bad, Mencken wasn't.

Everyone looks at him with surprise.

> CHARLES
> I submitted that article last week to the Baltimore Sun. Evidently, real newspapers aren't interested in small town hokum.

Rose sighs scoldingly. They've been over this before.

> ROSE
> Charles.
>
> MR. LEBARRON
> Well, okay, Mr. Big City Reporter. I've got a job for ya. William Jennings Bryan is speaking on the Butler Act tonight in Chattanooga. Why don't you cover it. And take Rose with you.
>
> CHARLES
> THE William Jennings Bryan?
>
> MR. LEBARRON
> (playfully)
> Three time Democratic presidential candidate Bryan. Leader of progressive causes and human rights. The one and only.
>
> CHARLES
> Thanks, Mr. LeBarron!

                    ROSE
          But I have to visit my sister.

Charles is already on his way out the door.

                    CHARLES
          It's on the way. We'll kill two birds with one
          stone.

EXT. SANITARIUM - DAY

Charles's Model T pulls into the driveway of the sanitarium and past the sign: "TENNESSEE COLONY FOR EPILEPTICS AND THE FEEBLEMINDED."

The Sanitarium is a stately reserve, resting calmly in the countryside, but a bit out of place.

INT. WOMEN'S GROUP LOUNGE, SANITARIUM - DAY

The large group lounge area contains a mixture of what appears to be normal women and mentally handicapped ones. Some, sleeping, some playing games, some in mindless oblivion, doing the "institutional rock."

A few NURSES and ORDERLIES go about their business helping patients or watching them. It's all peaceful and calm, but there's an unsettling eeriness to it all.

Over in the corner, ABIGAIL WILLIAMS (26) sits petting a cat with precious affection. Abigail is mentally retarded with the IQ of a 7 year old. And she is the most loving person you will ever meet.

She looks up and sees across the room: Charles and Rose, carrying a suitcase. Abigail's eyes light up with a smile.

                    ABIGAIL
          Rose!

In a flash, she is up and running to Rose. She slams into her with a bear hug that almost knocks her over, laughing.

And then Abigail moves to Charles, He hands her a couple of hand-picked flowers. She hugs him by surprise. He's a bit awkward with this all, but a good sport.

> ROSE
> (holding up the suitcase)
> I brought the rest of your things from the house.

Abigail turns a bit serious.

> ABIGAIL
> Rose, how long is my vacation going to be?

> ROSE
> I don't know, Abigail.

Rose holds back her emotions. Charles is distracted, looking around the room at everyone else.

> ROSE
> The doctors say they can take better care of you here than daddy can.

> ABIGAIL
> But I love daddy -- and I love you!

Rose grabs Abigail and hugs her again, like she'll never let go. Charles watches, uncomfortably.

> ROSE
> We love you, too, sweetie. And I'll be visiting you every week.

Charles looks at his pocket watch.

> CHARLES
> We should talk to the doctor.

INT. DOCTOR'S OFFICE, SANITARIUM - DAY

Rose sits in a chair listening to DR. HEYDRICH, a soft-spoken academic in a white doctor's lab coat, a trim scholarly beard, a slight German accent, and an empathetic charity. Charles stands behind her.

> DR. HEYDRICH
> Look, Miss Williams, I understand your concern. But I can assure you, Abigail is receiving the finest medical care from qualified professionals.

                    ROSE
Why can't I take care of her?

                    DR. HEYDRICH
Our research has shown that segregation is
healthier for the individual and society.

Rose looks at a pile of papers on the desk in front of her. In her hand, a pen for signing. Charles takes another look at his pocket watch.

                    CHARLES
We really should get going.

She looks at Charles. Then back to the papers. Not much choice. She signs the papers.

                    DR. HEYDRICH
Don't worry, Miss Williams. We provide the latest
and most scientifically proven methods of therapy
for your sister. You have to trust me.

Rose gives one last hesitant look at him, and finishes signing.

EXT. SANITARIUM - SUNSET

As they pull away from the sanitarium, Abigail stands in the doorway waving goodbye.

INT./EXT. MODEL T, DRIVING - SUNSET

Charles driving Rose. He's flapping off at the mouth, oblivious to the fact that Rose is too disheartened to be able to hear him.

                    CHARLES
The Butler Act makes it illegal to teach the
evolution of man in Tennessee schools. Problem is,
it's been in all the textbooks for years. And most
everybody's been teaching it for years. It's not a
question of whether there'll be a lawsuit. It's a
question of when. And who has the guts to
challenge the law. Bryan's a shrewd politician.
He'll probably be preaching to wealthy white

Southerners and industrialists to help line the pockets of his new campaign.

INT. BASEBALL STADIUM - EVENING

WILLIAM JENNINGS BRYAN (65) faces a crowd packed into a high school baseball stadium. He is a hearty man, balding, with intense eyes. He carries himself with confidence and authority, but also sincerity. A rare species: a politician with a conscience.

The speaker's platform faces the seats behind home plate. A large banner behind Bryan reads, "ANTI-EVOLUTION CRUSADE." A smaller banner reads, "NEGRO NIGHT."

> BRYAN
> Now, let me tell you about the menace of Darwinism...

Charles and Rose sit uncomfortably in the stands. The only white faces in a sea of African American families dressed smartly in suits and ties, dresses and hats.

> BRYAN
> The evolutionary theory represents man as reaching his present perfection by the operation of the law of hate - the merciless law by which the strong crowd out and kill off the weak...

Voices of disapproval ring through the crowd. Charles is busy taking notes. Rose is enraptured by Bryan.

> BRYAN
> And let me tell you, my friends. You are the target. Let me read to you the words of Charles Darwin himself...

He picks up a book and opens it to a dog-eared page and reads.

> BRYAN
> "At some future period, the civilized races of man will almost certainly exterminate and replace, the savage races throughout the world." And you are, to Mr. Darwin, I quote, "apish, and savage-like."

Now the crowd outright boos and hisses with passion.

> BRYAN
> Margaret Sanger says you are a "menace to the race." I quote: "We do not want word to go out that we want to exterminate the Negro population..."

Rose has her hand in horror over her mouth.

> BRYAN
> That, my beloved black brethren, is what these Social Darwinists think of you.

SILENCE grips the entire stadium. They are stunned by what they hear. Charles notices the dead quiet and looks around.

> BRYAN
> But not your Creator. He made you in his image. Made you of infinite value. And saved you from your sin - from the law of the jungle.

EXT. PARKING LOT, BASEBALL STADIUM - NIGHT

Bryan walks from the stadium with SEVERAL BLACK MINISTERS and his entourage. Charles approaches Bryan with his reporter's pad in hand. Rose follows apprehensively.

> CHARLES
> Mr. Bryan! I'm with the Dayton Herald! I have a few questions I'd like to ask you!

Bryan stops in his tracks with a curious look at Charles. His entourage almost runs into him from behind.

> BRYAN
> The press never covers a Negro religious event.

> CHARLES
> Well, sir, I'm trying to stand out from the herd.

Bryan warms up.

> BRYAN
> Be careful. Those are the ones the predators seek. So, how can I help you and your lovely companion?

Rose smiles.

> CHARLES
> Well, I was just wondering. You've been defeated now three times running for President. What if you've picked yet another losing cause with this anti-evolution crusade?

Bryan's warm smile drops, but he regains control.

> BRYAN
> Let me tell you something, son. God's truth is never a losing cause.

INT. THE BALTIMORE SUN NEWSPAPER OFFICE - DAY

Mencken sits on the ledge of his office looking out the window at a group of SUFFRAGETTES protesting the Newspaper with signs and marches two stories below.

MENCKEN'S POV: several women gather together, and from this high angle, the gathering is one of bosoms and cleavage. Mencken grins.

An EDITOR sticks his head in the office.

> EDITOR
> Keeping your eye on the Suffragette movement?

> MENCKEN
> From this angle it doesn't look too bad.

Mencken winks. The Editor smiles. Tosses an envelope on Mencken's desk.

> BALTIMORE SUN EDITOR
> That kid from Tennessee sent in another article. It's about Bryan and the evolution issue. It's pretty good.

Mencken ignores him. Keeps leering out the window. When the Editor is gone, Mencken picks up the envelope. Looks at it. Tosses it into the trash.

EXT. MARKET STREET, DAYTON - DAY

Charles and Rose walk down Market Street, the main road in town. They stop to watch a MERCHANT put a sign in his shop window, "GOING OUT OF BUSINESS." He pulls a shade and steps out the front door.

> CHARLES
> What's next, Mr. Peterman?

> MERCHANT
> Don't know. Gotta go someplace that's not shrinkin'. Up North, maybe.

Charles and Rose give each other an ominous look and continue on into the Drug Store.

INT. ROBINSON'S DRUG STORE - DAY

Charles and Rose sit at the counter and sip a couple of malted milks. Rose is troubled.

> CHARLES
> Abbie is in good hands. You did the right thing.

But Rose isn't encouraged. She turns thoughtful.

> ROSE
> When my mother left us, I just kept thinking it was my fault.

> CHARLES
> She went crazy, Rose. How can that be your fault?
> (beat)
> Maybe she'll come back some day.

> ROSE
> What if it runs in the family?

> CHARLES
> Don't be crazy.

Rose looks sharply at him. But then she sees his teasing look. And they finally share a chuckle.

Charles notices a group of men gathering with a conspiratorial hush. He sees a scrawny young man, JOHN SCOPES (24), carrying a football, being welcomed to the group.

> CHARLES
> Wait here, Rose. I'll be right back.

Rose watches Charles slip over near the group, behind a display of shopping goods. He pretends to look for something.

OVER BY THE CONSPIRACY

The four men at the table are: FRED "DOC" ROBINSON (60s), a pharmacist in a white coat; SUE HICKS (30) a male despite the female name, and an excitable type; RAPPLEYEA, a likeable New Yorker, but a stranger to Southern ways -- and an opportunist; and Scopes, a shy chain-smoker with horn-rimmed glasses. They surround a Chattanooga Times newspaper, held by Rappleyea.

> RAPPLEYEA
> Didn't I tell ya? The American Civil Liberties
> Union of New York is advertising to sponsor a test
> case challenging the anti-evolution law. They pay
> the costs and guarantee a friendly trial. And I
> might add I happen to know many of 'em
> personally.

The men are following with smiles.

> ROBINSON
> So if we get the case, we get the publicity.

> RAPPLEYEA
> Exactly! This'll put Dayton on the map,
> gentlemen! Turn our recession around!
>   (turns to Scopes)
> That's why you're here, Mr. Scopes. You teach
> biology, don't ya?

Scopes' face turns white.

SCOPES
Only as a substitute. I teach math and coach football.

Rappleyea pulls out a book and slams it on the table. It's "A CIVIC BIOLOGY by GEORGE HUNTER."

RAPPLEYEA
Is this the book you used in class?

SCOPES
Well, yes, but I never actually taught the section on evolution.

RAPPLEYEA
Technicality.

The men smile knowingly to each other.

Behind the display, Charles is still listening.

SCOPES
But I don't want to lose my job.

ROBINSON
John, I'm the Chairman of the School Board. You won't lose your job.

HICKS
And I'm a District Attorney. I could prosecute. It'll be among friends.

RAPPLEYEA
And I, gentlemen, will appropriate public relations. It's a corker. What do you say, Johnny?

Charles surprises them all, stepping out from behind the display.

CHARLES
And ya'll need a newspaper to carry your story to the rest of the world. This is national news.

Rappleyea's surprise turns to a grin. Can't argue with that. Rappleyea turns to Scopes.

                    RAPPLEYEA
You'll be famous.

                    SCOPES
But I don't want to be famous.

INT. THE DAYTON HERALD AND THE BALTIMORE SUN OFFICES - DAY

INTERCUT between Charles and Mencken on the phone in their respective offices.

                    MENCKEN
So the ACLU runs an ad for a willing teacher and you guys - the barber, the baker, the candlestick maker - have offered up your local yokel for sacrifice, do I have that right?

                    CHARLES
Yes, sir. The evolution debate is considerable in these parts. Maybe you read the story I sent you about it.

Silence on the other end. Mencken, his feet up, is eating a donut. He mouths the word, "No."

                    CHARLES
I've known these people all my life, sir. And I know John Scopes personally. I've got the inside scoop.

                    MENCKEN
Look, kid, this is not national news -- not yet, anyway. Rhea County is an out of the way backwater of illiterate farmers, superstitious Holy Rollers, and bucolic buncombe. -- No offense, of course.

                    CHARLES
Actually, sir, I agree with you. I'm only sticking around this podunk town because of the potential of this story, anyway.

                    MENCKEN
          If any national figures get involved, give me a call.
          Not before then.

Mencken hangs up without a goodbye. Charles grimaces. He looks over and pulls out a dictionary, muttering to himself.

                    CHARLES
          Bucolic buncombe. Bucolic buncombe.

EXT. LARGE WAREHOUSE IN CENTER OF DAYTON - DAY

Rappleyea and Robinson enter a beat-up warehouse in view of the Rhea County Courthouse.

INT. LARGE WAREHOUSE

The place looks like a tornado hit a junkyard. It's the secret repository of every single scrap item imaginable. Paper, boxes, rubber duckies, Oil drum cans, spare car parts. And five years of dust on everything. But Rappleyea sees past the trash -- to its possibilities. Robinson coughs.

                    RAPPLEYEA
          The Scopes Trial Entertainment Committee is
          fixing this place up for house reporters.

                    ROBINSON
          Boy, you work fast, Rapp.

                    RAPPLEYEA
          Have to.
               (confiding)
          I bought the 300 acres.

                    ROBINSON
          Wasn't that thirty thousand clams?

                    RAPPLEYEA
          I've got some investors from the hometown.

                    ROBINSON
          But we don't have the trial yet.

Rappleyea is smiling like a cat.

> RAPPLEYEA
> Technicality. This Yankee's got more than one way
> to scotch a snake.

INT. COUNTRY BAPTIST CHURCH - DAY

Rappleyea and Robinson are in the choir of the little country church singing a hymn.

In the pews, Rose happily sings next to Charles, who is not very engaged himself. He looks over and sees Hicks standing next to Scopes down the row, rather uninvolved in the service.

EXT. COUNTRY BAPTIST CHURCH - DAY

End of the service. Everyone leaving. Over on the grass, Rappleyea, Hicks, Robinson and Charles trying to be inconspicuous, glancing at their watches. Charles sees Rose talking with the Pastor.

PROFESSOR NEAL (42) approaches from the parking lot, led by Scopes. Neal is slovenly, unshaven and unkempt, this guy is truly the original nutty professor - but with an attitude.

> SCOPES
> This is the law professor from Knoxville I was
> telling y'all about. John Neal. He's an expert on
> Tennessee law.

> ROBINSON
> (friendly tongue in cheek)
> Missed you at the service, Professor.

> NEAL
> Yeah, well I don't believe in fairy tales.

Robinson's smile melts. Rappleyea gives a side-glance at Charles.

> RAPPLEYEA
> So, which side would you work best on, Neal?

> NEAL
> I told Scopes here, I'm on his defense whether he
> wants me or not.

Everyone chuckles nervously. Neal is not so lighthearted. Then they're interrupted by JUDGE RAULSTON (43), an optimistic good-natured Southern gentleman, with Southern etiquette.

> RAPPLEYEA
> Hey, Judge.

> NEAL
> Judge Raulston?

> JUDGE RAULSTON
> Yes, sir.

> NEAL
> Wouldn't this be a conflict of interest, if you judge the case?

Judge Raulston slaps him on the back.

> JUDGE RAULSTON
> Mr. Neal, we have a saying around here. What happens in church, stays in church. You might just call it "a separation of church and state."

The men snicker. Neal goes ahead.

> NEAL
> Well, I got some bad news.

He hands a newspaper to Rappleyea. Headline: "MONKEY TRIAL IN NASHVILLE?"

> NEAL
> Nashville's petitioning for the trial. They filed a violation of the anti-evolution statute.

> RAPPLEYEA
> Confederate bastards.

The men all stop and stare at him accusingly.

> RAPPLEYEA
> Sorry.

                    HICKS
They're trying to steal the trial out from under us.

                    JUDGE RAULSTON
Well, we're gonna steal it right back.

Everyone looks at Judge Raulston. Now, a scheming player.

                    JUDGE RAULSTON
I can move up the grand jury to indict Scopes this
week.

Scopes watches everyone quietly and helplessly, a pawn in their chess game.

                    CHARLES
                (jumping in)
That's not enough, sir.

Now all eyes on Charles.

                    CHARLES
We need a headliner in the papers -- fast.

They consider.

                    RAPPLEYEA
The boy's right. Someone on the case that will
bring national attention. Seal the deal.

Everyone agrees. But now Rappleyea and Charles reveal their hidden card. He nods to Charles, who pulls out a telegram from his pocket.

                    RAPPLEYEA
And we have just the man, gentlemen.

                    CHARLES
I got this yesterday.
                (reads)
"Received your wire. Happy to join the
prosecution. No charge."
                (milks it)
"William Jennings Bryan."

There is a stunned moment of silence. Rappleyea pulls out a cigar and lights it with a grin. Judge Raulston blurts out.

                    JUDGE RAULSTON
          PRAISE GOD!

Rose and other churchgoers nearby stop and turn their heads. Judge Raulston hushes up, embarrassed.

Charles grins victoriously. Scoop! He runs back over to Rose.

                    RAPPLEYEA
          Fellas, we got us a monkey trial.

Charles races right past Rose, who wonders where he is going.

INT. DAYTON HERALD OFFICES - DAY

Charles sits on the phone, waiting for an answer on the other line.

                    CHARLES
          Mr. Mencken? Charles Anderson with the Dayton
          Herald. I've got your national figure.

INT. CHICAGO STREETS - NIGHT

SUPER: CHICAGO

H.L. Mencken stands smoking a cigar outside the old row houses, looking out into the night.

                    MENCKEN
          There's a meeting in New York with the defense
          team. You need to be on this case.

He turns to speak. Behind him is Clarence Darrow.

                    MENCKEN
          This is big, Clarence. An opportunity to expose the
          dreadful bilge of religious ignoramuses.

Darrow smiles. Way with words.

                    DARROW
          What's your opinion of this Scopes fella?

                    MENCKEN
          I could care less about that yap of a schoolteacher.
          This is not about teaching evolution in the schools.

It's about who will control society: men of reason and enlightenment, or priests of superstition and hate. It's about science versus religion.

> DARROW
> Henry. The ACLU won't let me come near that defense with a ten foot pole. They're a bunch of Quakers and pacifists. They want a nice quiet legal strategy. And they certainly don't care for my atheism.

> MENCKEN
> To hell with the ACLU. Go straight to Scopes himself. He hires you, it's too late. You're in.

Darrow nods. Good point. But then he cools again. In his face, he lacks certainty.

> DARROW
> Who's on the prosecution team?

> MENCKEN
> Three names: William - Jennings - Bryan.

Darrow looks up at him with a delighted twinkle in his eye.

> DARROW
> I'll do it for free.

EXT. TRAIN TRACKS - DAY/NIGHT

Engineer's P.O.V.: MONTAGE of train tracks whizz by, first in daytime, then night. It's a long haul.

INT. NEW YORK CITY MANSION - NIGHT

SUPER: NEW YORK CITY

An elegant rich interior. Conspicuous consumption. Robber Barron wealth. Rockefeller mansion. A party for "old money" elite with gowns and tuxes.

Over in the corner, out of the way, stand Charles, Rappleyea, Scopes and Neal, very out of their element.

Rappleyea, happily munching away on a plateful of appetizers.

Scopes is uncomfortably shy, nervously smoking.

Neal, cynically detached, and still looking like a slob, even in a tux.

Charles is all wide-eyed ogling, taking it all in like a drug.

> CHARLES
> Is that him? Is that Rockefeller?

All their heads turn. An 86-year old ARISTOCRAT, flanked by TWO BODYGUARDS, speaks to a small group.

> NEAL
> Enjoy the view, Johnny Rebs. You'll never be this
> close again to the top of the food chain.

Every one of them but Neal has their mouths agape.

> MENCKEN
> Shut your jaws. You look like a bunch of drooling
> apes.

They all turn to see Mencken standing there with a big cigar in his chops. With him are Clarence Darrow and DUDLEY MALONE (30s), debonair and acting like a dandy with an Irish brogue.

> MENCKEN
> Okay, you corn-pone country lawyers. This is
> Clarence Darrow and his law partner, Dudley
> Malone. Dudley is a divorced, lapsed Catholic.
> Clarence is an infidel heretic, and they're your last
> best hope against the mob of unevolved village
> idiots. Or as I like to call them, "homo boobiens."

The defense team chuckles nervously.

> DARROW
> Thanks for the affectionate introduction, Henry.

Now their laughs loosen a bit with Darrow's soft touch. Darrow and Malone exchange handshakes and names with each one.

Charles draws Mencken's attention aside. Offers his hand.

CHARLES
Mr. Mencken. I'm Charles Anderson.

Mencken doesn't appear to recognize the name.

CHARLES
The Dayton Herald?

Now Mencken's eyes light up. But then, turn suspicious.

MENCKEN
Who let you in the chicken coop?

CHARLES
I'm a rooster, sir. Just looking for the fox.

Mencken eyes him, impressed with the perseverance. Takes a puff. Sees a waiter walking by with a tray. Grabs two glasses off it.

MENCKEN
Cognac.

Charles doesn't take it. He's uncomfortable.

CHARLES
(haltingly)
Prohibition, sir. It's illegal.

MENCKEN
We're in the Rockefeller mansion, boy. Safe in the bowels of wealth and privilege. "Above the laws of lesser mortals."

He takes a delicious sip. Charles doesn't budge. Mencken chuckles with condescension.

MENCKEN
So, you wanna be a big city reporter, huh?

CHARLES
Yes, sir.

MENCKEN
Let me give you your first lesson of survival in the laws of the jungle. The biggest lion doesn't have to

follow the laws of the jungle. Nietzsche called it,
"beyond good and evil."

He offers the glass again. But Charles sighs. Just can't do it.

MENCKEN
For God's sake, at least hold the damn thing, so I
can smoke my cigar.

Charles grabs the glass apologetically. Mencken turns back to the lawyers.

CHARLES
Sir.
(Mencken stops)
I gave you the Bryan story.

Mencken pauses.

MENCKEN
You're right, kid.

He reaches in his pocket, pulls out a cigar, and hands it to Charles.

MENCKEN
Consider us even. Keep up the good work.

CHARLES
But I don't...

MENCKEN
Don't tell me. You don't smoke. I tell you what.
When you make it big, then smoke the cigar in my
honor. But until you can get me any inside dirt on
Bryan, you're still just a stringer to me, kid.

Darrow interrupts.

DARROW
I can tell you about Bryan, Henry. I campaigned
for him in the Democratic Party.

All eyes turn to Darrow who is deadly serious. It's like he's around a campfire, talking about facing a dangerous predator.

                    DARROW
         He never forgets a face. He never forgets a name.
         And when he talks to you in a crowded room,
         you're the only person in the world.

The crowd gets quieter.

                    DARROW
         But he is an absolutely dangerous man. When he
         speaks, the sun shines, the wind dies down, and
         the neighbor's dog stops barking. It's a summer
         for the gods. You lean forward...
              (His voice lowers)
         and you want with all your heart to believe that he
         actually can save the world. Except... except that
         none of it is true. And you realize you've been
         played.

The room is quiet. Darrow drags on his cigarette.

                    MENCKEN
         Sounds like you, Clarence.

Darrow looks at Mencken and, with a smile and hoist of his glass, tosses back his Cognac.

EXT. DAYTON - DAY

THE TOWN IS GETTIN' READY FOR THE BIG TRIAL:

Painters paint several storefronts on Market Street.

Mr. Peterman, the dejected merchant from earlier, happily removes his "GOING OUT OF BUSINESS" sign. Replaces it with a new one: "OPEN FOR BUSINESS."

Vendors are setting up their stands up and down Market Street. Everything from food to literature pamphleteering.

A banner: "ANTI-EVOLUTION LEAGUE: HELL AND THE HIGH SCHOOL."

Construction men build a stage outside the county courthouse, along with benches, and section the area off with flagged rope.

Inside the courthouse, a team of technical sound men put up a booth with special microphones under the logo of WGN RADIO.

In his home, Scopes dumps a duffle bag of mail on his floor. He is surrounded by bags of mail.

Charles is standing by his car, watching a small passenger aircraft land on a homemade airstrip near town.

Mencken exits the open door of the airplane. Sees Charles.

Mr. LeBarron and his wife pound in two yard signs: "WELCOME MR. BRYAN!" and "WELCOME MR. DARROW!" The LeBarrons finish their pounding in time to watch Charles's car drive by. A cigar butt is tossed from the passenger seat and lands in their yard.

INT. CHARLES'S AUTOMOBILE DRIVING - DAY

Charles has the cigar from New York in his pocket as he navigates the road. Mencken lights up a fresh cigar in the back seat.

> MENCKEN
> Let's take a look at your writing, greenhorn.

He opens a folder in his lap, and scans articles. Each statement he makes hits Charles like a bullet.

> MENCKEN
> Incurably sentimental.
> (looks at another)
> Pathetically puritan.
> (looks at another)
> Bucolic buncombe.

Charles snaps his eyes to the rear view mirror. He knows that one.

> MENCKEN
> But you do show promise, kid.
> (self-amused)
> Kinda like Mowgli. The jungle child seeking civilization.

Charles rolls his eyes, unseen by Mencken.

> MENCKEN
> You got passion, persistence. But you need wit. It's what separates you from the gorillas, Mowgli. The

great masses of inferiors called "the common man."

(holds up an article)
I don't want to read about some Strawberry Queen's procession down Main Street. Tell me about her sex life.

CHARLES
But isn't that yellow journalism?

MENCKEN
It's called "entertainment."

CHARLES
What about the facts?

MENCKEN
Facts are boring, Mowgli. Give me the truth.

Charles drives on, pondering his teacher's wisdom.

EXT. DAYTON MARKET STREET WAREHOUSE - DAY

Charles's car pulls up to the warehouse. Freshly painted and repaired, it has been transformed with a sign: "PRESS ACCOMMODATIONS."

INT. DAYTON MARKET STREET WAREHOUSE - DAY

Charles, carrying Mencken's suitcase, leads Mencken in. They stop to see the room is cleaned out of its previous junk and now filled with cots, like a military barracks. Several reporters have already set up travel trunks by their beds for night-stands. Mencken does not look pleased.

Rappleyea busily greets other reporters. He sees Mencken across the room and bellows obnoxiously, waving his hand.

RAPPLEYEA
Mr. Mencken! Mr. Mencken, welcome to Dayton!

Everyone stops and looks at Mencken and Charles at the door. Mencken whispers under his breath to Charles.

MENCKEN
Who's that clown?

Almost as if Rappleyea hears him...

> RAPPLEYEA
> George Rappleyea! Head of the Scopes Trial Entertainment Committee!

> MENCKEN
> (smirking)
> Oh, this is going to be hog heaven.

Rappleyea gives a piercing two-fingered whistle and addresses the crowd of reporters.

> RAPPLEYEA
> Can I have your attention please! We don't have the toilet quite hooked-up yet, so you'll have to use the outhouse out back.

Mencken rolls his eyes. He's just about had it.

> RAPPLEYEA
> Oh, and there's some real estate for sale around here! Great place to settle down, Dayton!
> (aside)
> If you could work that into one of your stories...

Mencken and Charles look at each other amused. Charles looks around as Mencken picks up his bag and walks right back out the way he came. Charles looks back surprised. Runs to catch up with Mencken...

EXT. DAYTON MARKET STREET WAREHOUSE - DAY

Charles catches up with the briskly walking Mencken.

Mencken stops. Sees a nice hotel across the street.

> MENCKEN
> Now, that's more like it.
> (to Charles)
> Another rule of journalism, Mowgli: If you run with the herd, you're just another member of the herd.

And Mencken is off for the hotel, with Charles close behind.

EXT. DAYTON TRAIN STATION - DAY

A passenger train pulls into the station. A band starts playing "O When the Saints Come Marching In." A large crowd awaits Bryan's arrival. It includes Rappleyea, Hicks, Charles and Mencken.

Bryan steps out of the "Royal Palm Limited" coach amidst applause. He helps MRS. BRYAN (58) off the train in her wheelchair. She is attractive, gray-haired and visibly arthritic. Bryan puts a white pith helmet on his balding head.

Rappleyea hands Bryan a "Welcome to Dayton" pamphlet to his amusement. Bryan looks down to see A LITTLE GIRL offering him a paper sack. Bryan stops everything to notice this little cutie. He kneels down to her level and peeks inside the bag.

                BRYAN
Radishes?

                LITTLE GIRL
I have diabetes, just like you, Mr. Bryan. My daddy tells me to eat radishes, 'cause they're good for me. But they taste yucky.

Bryan takes a bite of one. Winces at the bitterness. Smiles.

                BRYAN
You're right. They're yucky. But sometimes, sweetheart, the thing we don't like is the best thing for us. So I'll make sure to eat plenty of these.

Bryan hugs the Little Girl. The Crowd responds with "Awws."

In the crowd, Mencken sarcastically editorializes to Charles.

                MENCKEN
That's why they call him "the Great Commoner."
Hearts of the yokels in his hands.

Charles gets an idea. Pulls away from Mencken to get closer to Bryan. Mencken watches him with piqued curiosity.

Bryan stands up to address the crowd.

BRYAN

Thank you one and all for such a warm reception. Mrs. Bryan and I are truly grateful.

He holds Mrs. Bryan's hand lovingly. She smiles and nods in agreement. Applause from all.

BRYAN

And let me assure you, this is not a minor legal squabble you have here in the good city of Dayton. This is a battle royale, a duel to the death!

More applause. Bryan tries to move along, but Charles speaks out from the crowd.

CHARLES

Mr. Bryan!

Bryan gives his attention.

CHARLES

You once said God's truth is not a losing cause. But how does God measure up when all the experts and scientists are on the side of evolution?

Mencken smiles, impressed with Charles's bravado.

Bryan stares at Charles with curiosity. Then he lights up with warm recognition.

BRYAN

I remember you. How ya doin', Charles?

CHARLES
(embarrassed)

Fine.

BRYAN

Well, let me just say, Charles, that the battle is not between science and religion. The battle is between democracy and aristocracy. Who will control the education, and therefore the minds, of young people: the majority of Americans or the minority of elitists who consider themselves above

the common man? I contend that the hand that
writes the paycheck rules the school.

The crowd agrees with cheers and applause.

Mencken rolls his eyes in contempt.

Applause continues. Hicks steps up to Bryan and introduces himself, picking up the Bryan's luggage.

INT. CHARLES'S AUTOMOBILE - DAY

Hicks and another man, McKENZIE (75), folksy, unsophisticated Southern gentleman, drive Bryan and Mrs. Bryan into Dayton. Lawn signs and strawberry stands dot the road into town.

                HICKS
Mr. Bryan, this is Ben McKenzie. He's on our team.

McKenzie turns to nod at Bryan.

                HICKS
He's argued before the Supreme Court.

Bryan looks impressed.

                MCKENZIE
The way, I see it, Colonel Bryan, we are bein' baited to turn this trial into a national seminar on evolution. Now, my thought is to keep creation and evolution outta that courtroom like a hound with the heaves.

                BRYAN
Why is that, counsel?

                HICKS
Well, sir. To be honest, we just don't have the experts to match theirs.

                BRYAN
What about George McReady Price? Howard Kelly at Johns Hopkins?

                    HICKS
          Price is in England, and Kelly has some
          questionable theories that make him a liability.
          Quite frankly, sir, when it comes to experts, we're
          outnumbered and outgunned.

Bryan sighs with frustration.

                    BRYAN
          No doubt, they'll paint us out to be uneducated
          hillbillies.

                    MCKENZIE
          I say we stick with a strictly legal strategy. The law
          says it's illegal to teach the theory of evolution. All
          we gotta do is prove Scopes taught it, and we go
          to the jury. Guilty as a garter. Sell some lemonade,
          "Thank you very much. Y'all come down and visit
          us again real soon."

Bryan appears troubled. The car pulls into the driveway of a home.

                    HICKS
          Here's your rental during the trial, Mr. and Mrs.
          Bryan.

Mrs. Bryan looks out the window. It's a humble residence.

                    MRS. BRYAN
          Thank you for your generous hospitality, Mr.
          Hicks.

EXT. MEADOW OUTSIDE DAYTON- DAY

Charles and Rose sit on a picnic blanket with a food spread around them. Rose affectionately watches Abigail chasing butterflies. Charles is caught up in himself.

                    CHARLES
          I don't understand it. I've done everything he's
          asked and more. But he still won't hire me.

ROSE
D'ya think Mr. Mencken might be using you?

CHARLES
If I don't get this break, I'll probably be stuck in Dayton for the rest of my life.

ROSE
I can think of worse things.

Charles finally hears her. Gives an apologetic smile.

ROSE
What do you really fear, Charles?

Charles thinks about it.

CHARLES
I guess I fear becoming like my father.

ROSE
Your father was a good man.

CHARLES
He was an ordinary man. Never wanting to rise above – insignificance.

ROSE
He married a good woman. Raised a good son. Started the Dayton Herald. Isn't that significant?

This hits home. Charles smiles. A light of new excitement floods over him.

CHARLES
Rose. It's a new world outside the hills and fields of this small town. A world that's advancing and developing into something our parents never dreamed of. And I want to be a part of it. I want to be significant in a way that my father never was. And I want you to go there with me. Marry me, Rose.

> ROSE
> Charles Anderson, you are a dreamer. But I do believe, in this small town, we still believe in traditional tokens of promise.

Charles's face goes blank. Is she turning him down? Then it hits him.

> CHARLES
> A ring! I know, a ring. I'm so sorry. I'll get a ring. I just...

> ROSE
> And I can't think of anything more I'd rather do, than dream with you.

Charles smiles. Moves to kiss her...

But Abigail is there with a big frog in her hand. It croaks.

> ABIGAIL
> Mr. Charles! Look what I found!

And the frog jumps out of her hands into Rose's lap. She screams and jerks away. But the frog jumps out of her lap and the three of them have a good laugh together. Suddenly, Charles remembers something. Pulls out his pocket watch.

> CHARLES
> Oh, no. I forgot. I'm supposed to be at the train station.

They rush to pick up the blanket and food.

EXT. DAYTON TRAIN STATION - DAY

Rappleyea, Neal and Mencken watch a train coach car, waiting.

> MENCKEN
> There he is, "The Lawyer of the Damned."

Darrow steps off the train with Malone, surprised at the cheering crowd. The band strikes up "Battle Hymn of the Republic." Darrow looks confused. Yells in Mencken's ears.

> DARROW
> Don't these people know who I am?

                    MENCKEN
    Prey never recognizes its predator until it's too
    late.

Darrow laughs and shakes hands with greeters.

INT./EXT. AUTOMOBILE AT THE MANSION- DAY

Rappleyea drives Darrow, Malone, and Neal up to a huge wealthy-looking mansion.

                    RAPPLEYEA
    This here's your headquarters for the defense, Mr.
    Darrow.

                    DARROW
    Well, you can tell Henry not everyone in the town
    of Dayton is a poor yokel from the sticks.

Everyone laughs, but Rappleyea is a bit uncomfortable.

EXT. TRAIN STATION - DAY

It's empty. No one around. Charles stands dejected. He missed his opportunity.

EXT. TRAIN STATION PARKING - DAY

Charles walks up to his car, where Rose and Abigail wait for him. Rose can see he is down.

                    ROSE
    I'm so sorry, Charles.

                    CHARLES
            (to Rose)
    Why don't you just bring Abigail back to the
    home. I'm gonna go into town and see if I can find
    Mr. Mencken.

Rose slides over to take the wheel. He weakly kisses her on the cheek. He turns around and mopes his way toward Market Street. Rose watches him with sympathy before she pulls away.

                    ABIGAIL
    Mr. Charles looks sad.

                              ROSE
                He's just a little disappointed, that's all.

                              ABIGAIL
                With who?

Rose doesn't answer. She drives away.

EXT. MARKET STREET DAYTON - DAY

Downtown Dayton has turned into a festival. There are booths for fundamentalists, suffragettes, prohibitionists, anti-evolutionists, hot dogs, lemonade, and of course a million monkey trinkets. Stuffed toy monkeys are everywhere.

A storefront: J.R. DARWIN CLOTHIER, with other signs: "OUR CLOTHES ARE THE FITTEST," and "DARWIN IS RIGHT... INSIDE."

A banner is being hoisted over Market Street: "WELCOME TO THE MONKEY TRIAL."

Another banner over Robinson's Drug Store: "ROBINSON'S DRUG STORE: WHERE IT ALL STARTED."

A Policeman's motorcycle with a sign: "MONKEYVILLE POLICE."

A TRAINER leads a trained chimpanzee, JOE MENDI, dressed up in a little plaid suit, in doing some silly dancing for a crowd of giggling children. His sign: JOE MENDI: MASCOT OF MONKEYTOWN.

One large exhibit on a hay wagon is sponsored by the Bronx Zoo and has a big poster of the evolution of the horse: Eohippus to the modern day horse.

But the highlight of the exhibit are full-scale realistic figurines of mankind's ancestry: Java, Nebraska, Piltdown, Heidelberg, Neanderthal. The littlest children keep their distance. The ZOO CURATOR points to Piltdown.

                              CURATOR
                Piltdown Man, the missing link! The most solid
                proof of evolution that proves creationism is a
                hoax!

Now he points to Nebraska Man.

CURATOR
Nebraska Man, authenticated by leading scientists and recreated here with perfect anatomical accuracy based on a tooth found only a few years ago in the state of Nebraska. Practically in Bryan's back yard!

The crowd laughs. He points to a detailed drawing of a family of Nebraska ape men imaginatively socializing.

CURATOR
And here is what his family looked like. Accurately rendered by our scientific artists.

OVER BY ANOTHER BOOTH

A large banner, "DECK CARTER: BIBLE CHAMPION OF THE WORLD." Behind CARTER is a stack of Bibles. Onlookers move in. Carter stares directly at Mencken across from him.

CARTER
That's right, Mr. Mencken. Any verse in the entire Bible. If you can start it, I can finish it. Or you get your money back and a prize to boot.

Mencken slaps down a dime and picks up the Bible. He closes his eyes, opens to the middle of the book, and plants his finger. Opening his eyes, he starts the verse:

MENCKEN
"He that troubleth ..."

CARTER
"He that troubleth his own house shall inherit the wind." Proverbs 11:29.

The crowd is amazed. Several slap their knees.

CHARLES
Mr. Mencken!

Mencken turns. Charles walks up to him.

CARTER
...and the fool shall be servant to the wise of heart."

CHARLES
I'm so sorry. I don't know what happened. I was with my girlfriend and the time got away from me.

MENCKEN
That's all real sweet and sticky. But every story has two sides, and you missed the most important one this afternoon.

Mencken turns on his heels and walks over to a booth. It's a large tented exhibit. The sign: "REAL LIVE MISSING LINK! COME INSIDE!" Charles chases him.

CHARLES
You're right, sir. I won't let it happen again.

MENCKEN
Too little, too late.

Mencken enters. Charles enters behind him. He ain't givin' up.

INT. MISSING LINK EXHIBIT

Charles chases Mencken through the dark hallway leading to the display.

CHARLES
Please, sir. Give me another chance. I won't let you down again.

MENCKEN
You let yourself down.

They stop by the bars of a cage. It's dark all around except for some key lighting on the cage bars.

MENCKEN
Your priorities are backwards.

Suddenly out of the darkness, a three foot tall, WILD PYGMY, jumps at the bars right by them and scares the daylights out of them. A BARKER yells out.

                    BARKER
          Feast your eyes on the missing link of evolution! A
          pygmy seized on safari in the darkest regions of
          Africa!

                    MENCKEN
              (to Charles)
          Sorry, Mowgli. City's just too big for a jungle boy
          like you.

And Mencken leaves Charles in the dust, looking sadly at the Pygmy, who looks sadly back at him.

INT. BRYAN RENTED RESIDENCE, DAYTON - EVENING

Mr. and Mrs. Bryan sit before a fireplace in the modest den. She is in her wheelchair beside him on the couch. He gently rubs cream into her arthritic hands.

                    MRS. BRYAN
          I worry about you, William. Traveling hither and
          yon. Always trying to save the world. You're not
          40 years old anymore.

                    BRYAN
          Now, now, Mother.

She looks closer.

                    MRS. BRYAN
          You look troubled.

He pauses. Can't hide anything from this woman.

                    BRYAN
          Mr. Darrow. He's quite a formidable adversary.
          And he's got the experts on his side.

                    MRS. BRYAN
          William, sometimes I think you think you need to
          have all the answers or God just can't win.

He smiles to himself. She's right.

                    BRYAN
There's going to be no discussion of evolution or
the Bible. The issue is simply whether Scopes
broke the law or not.

                    MRS. BRYAN
Isn't that a good legal strategy?

                    BRYAN
That's not what I came for. I came to debate the
big issues, not legal details.
          (worried)
I haven't done law in years.

                    MRS. BRYAN
William, don't be such a cripple.

He looks at her with surprise. Then they both realize what she just said, and they laugh.

INT. THE MANSION - NIGHT

It's quite the posh residence of luxury. Darrow and gang have worked up the den area into their makeshift headquarters. Tables, papers, phones and law texts. Cigarette smoke hangs in the air. Darrow paces, smoking. Malone and Neal sit at the paper filled tables, also smoking.

                    NEAL
We have eleven lined up to testify. All of them,
experts in their fields of science. We'll bury the
prosecution.

A funny thought hits Malone.

                    MALONE
Too bad you can't get ol' Bryan up there on the
stand.

                    DARROW
I'd gut him like a fish.

Malone and Darrow share a smirk. Neal is not amused.

                    DARROW
    I've been waiting for an opportunity like this for
    years. Ever since that old blunderbuss challenged
    me in the papers.

                    NEAL
    Excuse me, but it's Scopes who's on trial, here.

Darrow looks into a roaring fireplace. And the roaring fireplace looks into Darrow.

                    DARROW
    No. Scopes is not on trial. Civilization is on trial.
    Nothing will satisfy me but a complete extinction
    of morons and their idol of morondom, Bryan
    himself. I want a knockout with an everlasting
    precedent to prove that America is founded on
    liberty and not on narrow, mean, intolerable, and
    brainless prejudice of soulless religious maniacs.

Neal sighs with frustration and slams the table.

                    NEAL
    This is exactly why the ACLU didn't want you on
    this case! Don't turn this into your circus,
    Clarence!

Clarence stands still, his back to them. Malone looks fearfully at Neal. What's he gonna do? Then, Darrow slowly turns around and with a sly devilish twinkle in his eye...

                    DARROW
    Gentlemen, I think it's time to talk about a strategy
    to dismiss the trial. After all, we don't want this
    thing turning into a - circus.

INT. HOTEL AQUA - NIGHT

Mencken approaches his room and fiddles with his keys.

                    LEBARRON
    Mr. Mencken!

Mencken looks up. Sees LeBarron rushing to him down the hall with a photograph in his hand.

> MENCKEN
> Sorry, no autographs.

> LEBARRON
> That's not why I'm here. I want to talk to you about Charles Anderson.

Mencken's face turns sour.

> LEBARRON
> He's a very fine writer, Mr. Mencken. Best I've worked with.

> MENCKEN
> Who has the priorities of his local gene pool.

> LEBARRON
> Hasn't anyone ever given you a second chance?

This makes Mencken consider. But not really…

> MENCKEN
> Haven't you heard of natural selection? The fit survive, the unfit perish.

> LEBARRON
> What about heredity and common ancestry?

Mencken is not following. LeBarron shows him the photograph. It's of a collegiate Mencken with another YOUNG MAN posing as buddies.

> LEBARRON
> I believe that's you and Jack Anderson. Polytechnic Institute? Class of '96?

And for the first time, Mencken is thrown off balance.

> MENCKEN
> His father?

LeBarron gives a tight-lipped "yes" look at him.

INT. AQUA HOTEL HALLWAY - NIGHT

Charles plods down the hallway noting the room numbers. Finally, he stops at Mencken's room. Composes himself. Takes a deep nervous breath. Goes to knock. Stops. Can't do it. Okay, let's get this over with. He knocks weakly.

> MENCKEN
> (behind the door)
> Door's open!

Charles awkwardly opens the door. Inside is Mencken, sitting in his underwear, with big bold circular glasses, smoking an Old Willie cigar, and typing away on his worn out Corona typewriter. Charles fidgets uncomfortably at the sight. Mencken keeps typing.

> CHARLES
> You called for me, sir?

> MENCKEN
> Shut the door.

Charles shuts the door hesitantly. Mencken keeps typing.

> MENCKEN
> I gotta admit, kid, I was a bit too harsh on you.

Charles nods slightly.

> MENCKEN
> Hell no. I was a horse's ass.

The humility shocks Charles.

> MENCKEN
> Okay, look, you got the job.

Charles's eyes widen.

> MENCKEN
> You'll work on supplements first thing tomorrow.
> I'll edit, teach you the ropes. No promises.

> CHARLES
> No sir.

                    MENCKEN
          But if you impress me by the end of this freak
          show, maybe I'll give you a job at the Sun.

Charles is wide mouthed. Can't believe it. Mencken rips the paper out of his Corona. Stands up.

                    MENCKEN
          Don't stand there like a gaping primate. Get your
          dancing shoes on, Mowgli. We're gonna celebrate.
          And bring that skirt of yours.

EXT. DAYTON BACK ALLEY - NIGHT

A spiffed up Mencken, Charles and Rose walk down a dark quiet alley behind Market Street.

                    CHARLES
          Where are we going? All the businesses are closed
          at this hour.

                    MENCKEN
          Not this business.

They step up to a back door, guarded by a big BOUNCER. The Bouncer stands aside and lets them in.

INT. SPEAKEASY - NIGHT

It's a smoke-filled, low-lit makeshift speakeasy. Cotton Club Jazz. Loaded with reporters and any other "in the know" out-of-towners.

Mencken drags Charles and Rose through the masses of partygoers over to the corner, where Darrow sits with his arm around a sexy FLAPPER with a cigarette and cocktail in her hand. Neal and Malone are at the table with dates as well.

                    DARROW
          Henry! There you are, you old curmudgeon!
               (sees Charles and Rose)
          Those your children?

Charles and Rose look suspiciously out of place, like they are his children.

                    MENCKEN
    This is that young buck I was telling you about,
    and his tomato.

Charles moves forward to shake Darrow's hand.

                    CHARLES
    Hello, sir, it's nice to meet you and your wife.

Darrow looks at the Flapper. Winks at Charles.

                    DARROW
    Only for tonight, son.

Charles is taken aback. Awkwardly gestures to Rose.

                    CHARLES
    My fiancé, Rose.

Rose gives an uncomfortable wave. Darrow nods back. Rose coughs at the hanging smoke. Darrow offers one of several liquor-filled glasses to Mencken.

                    DARROW
    Have some hooch, Henry! One thing about these
    backwoods mountain men, they sure bootleg some
    nasty bathtub gin!

Henry takes it, toasts and guzzles it. Charles and Rose are really unsettled with the environment. Mencken salutes.

                    MENCKEN
    To the ombibulous mountain men!

The Flappers look at each other ignorantly. Then to Darrow, who shrugs. He doesn't know what it means either.

Charles turns down a drink. Mencken winks at Darrow.

                    MENCKEN
    Puritan guilt.

Darrow gives Charles, an "is that a fact?" look.

                    DARROW
    The good book says, "Stolen water is sweeter!"

                    MENCKEN
Never forget, Mowgli, all the great villainies of
history have been perpetrated by sober men and
teetotalers.

                    CHARLES
Actually, sir, the trial starts tomorrow and I was
thinking we better get back and get some sleep.
Our first big day and all.

                    MENCKEN
Suit yourself. Don't forget to shut the door behind
you. Don't want any Holy Rollers finding their
way in and spoiling all the fun!

                    DARROW
Hallelujah!

Everyone around him laughs. Mencken belches ferociously.

EXT. RHEA COUNTY COURTHOUSE, DAYTON - DAY

The sun burns with scorching intensity. Crowds of people are lined up in two lines to enter the courthouse. Whites on the right, blacks on the left. A BAILIFF holds them at bay.

ON DARROW AND HIS TEAM

Darrow, Neal, Scopes and Malone march up past the lines and into the courthouse. They all squint and look like death with a hangover, except Scopes. Malone wipes sweat from his brow.

                    MALONE
Where did this heat wave come from?

                    NEAL
              (teasing)
You think God might be trying to stop us?

                    DARROW
Let him. I'll serve him with a subpoena and nail
him on the witness stand.

They all laugh as they enter the building past the two lines of waiting people. The whites up front are clean cut, eyeing the blacks with disdain.

Judge Raulston walks up to the Bailiff. He's decked out in a three piece suit. No robes here.

> BAILIFF
> Mornin', Judge.

> JUDGE RAULSTON
> Mornin', James.

Judge Raulston sees the young white men. Scowls when he sees the LEAD, a particularly sinewy one, with a snake head.

> JUDGE RAULSTON
> I know you boys. I know you in the Klan. Ya'll go on home, now. I don't want no trouble in my court.

Snakehead turns sour. Looks at the blacks across the way.

> SNAKEHEAD
> You gonna kick us out. But you gonna let them jigaboos in?

> JUDGE RAULSTON
> You heard what I said.

Snakehead doesn't move. But then from behind comes a hearty voice...

> BRYAN
> There a problem here, judge?

All eyes turn to see Bryan in his white pith helmet, pushing Mrs. Bryan's wheelchair, followed by Hicks and McKenzie. Bryan stares straight at Judge Raulston.

> BRYAN
> I do hope there will be no delay in allowing these fine upstanding citizens from entering the courthouse.

Judge Raulston glances at the whites. Is he talking about these brigands?

But Bryan walks up to the blacks and puts an arm around one of their shoulders. Looks with contempt over at the Klan kids.

> BRYAN
> Because you see, there are too many wild animals out in the street. And being a pacifist, I don't want to have to shoot 'em.

Snakehead hisses and turns, leading his miscreants away, with a distinct limp in his step. Bryan shakes some black's hands and carries Mrs. Bryan in her wheelchair up the steps with the help of McKenzie and Hicks. Snakehead keeps looking back with bitterness as he limps away.

INT. RHEA COUNTY COURTHOUSE - DAY

People squeeze into the steaming Rhea County Courthouse. Many wave palm leaf fans. A small corner in the very back for blacks.

Malone is dressed in a snappy suit. Darrow, his jacket off, wears purple suspenders over a lavender shirt. Neal is disheveled, and Scopes nervous and smoking.

Over in the press box, Charles looks around like an eager puppy. Next to him, Mencken is rubbing his temple and nursing a hangover, wiping his sweaty forehead with a handkerchief.

Charles notices Rose in the back. She waves lovingly to him. He smiles.

> MENCKEN
> Will you stop jerking around like a squirrel?

> CHARLES
> Sorry. Oh, I wanted to ask. Can my fiancé be our stenographer? She's a fast typist.

> MENCKEN
> Sure. Aren't there any fans in this hell hole?

> CHARLES
> The yokels haven't invented one yet.

Mencken looks up at him. They share a smile.

And then a commotion arises at the back. Charles jerks around to see Bryan entering the courtroom with his team. Flash powder goes off. Bryan walks through the crowd shaking hands, all smiles. Applause breaks out. A standing ovation.

Over by the defense table, Darrow and company roll their eyes and shake their heads.

Over by Charles and Mencken.

> MENCKEN
> Let the orgy of imbeciles begin.

Over by the special WGN Booth, a RADIO ANNOUNCER blathers into his microphone.

> WGN RADIO ANNOUNCER
> Arriving in the courtroom on this blistering hot day, for the first trial ever broadcast in America, is the religious fundamentalist, William Jennings Bryan. Looking tired and worn out, compared to Darrow's strong youthful vigor.

Bryan and his team make their way up to the defense table before stopping at their own. Darrow stands up. Bryan gives him a huge friendly smile.

> BRYAN
> Colonel. It is an honor to be your adversary.

He offers a friendly hand. Darrow hesitates with a touch of contempt. But gives in. They shake to a new outbreak of applause and camera flashes. Bryan and team finds their way to the prosecution table.

The Bailiff bellows:

> BAILIFF
> All rise!

Judge Raulston enters, the crowd rises, cameras pop.

> BAILIFF
> Oyez, oyez, oyez!

JUDGE RAULSTON

The Court will come to order. In view of the stifling heat, coats may be dispensed with...

Just about everyone in the courthouse whips off their jackets in unison, including the Prosecution and Defense. But Malone keeps his on.

JUDGE RAULSTON

...as well as, I'm afraid, all smoking tobacco.

There is some grumbling. A farmer with an enormous bulge in his cheek gets a dirty look from his wife.

JUDGE RAULSTON (O.S.)

Chewing will be allowed.

The farmer gives his wife her look back. Spits in a spittoon at his feet with a satisfied smile.

UP BY THE DEFENSE AND PROSECUTION

Both sides take off their jackets, except Malone.

JUDGE RAULSTON

The Rev. Cartwright will open with prayer.

All heads bow.

DARROW

I object.

The crowd is aghast. Hicks cannot believe it. Bryan shakes his head knowingly. The Judge looks confused at Darrow.

DARROW

Given the nature of this case we think that prayers offered under the auspices of the Court are prejudicial to our client.

Now Hicks hops up, steaming.

HICKS

And we think that such a suggestion as has been extended by the atheistic counsel for the Defense is foreign to the entire history of American legal

>   jurisprudence. That is, unless Mr. Darrow is trying
> to turn this court into a Soviet state.

The crowd cheers. Darrow glares spitefully. The Judge raps his gavel. Darrow takes the lead, looking at Hicks.

>   DARROW
>   I would like to correct the prosecution on his
>   ignorance. I am not an atheist, I am an agnostic.

Mencken smiles deviously. He knows better. Some of the crowd laughs at the comeback. Bryan whispers to Hicks.

>   BRYAN
>   In public.

>   JUDGE RAULSTON
>   Colonel Darrow, I have always opened my Court
>   with prayer in the past and see no compelling
>   reason to depart from that practice today.
>   (to Cartwright)
>   Reverend?

As Cartwright prays, Darrow, Neal and Mencken continue to look up, defiantly.

>   REV. CARTWRIGHT
>   Oh, God, our Divine Father, we recognize Thee as
>   the Supreme Ruler of the Universe and approach
>   unto Thy province this morning with that degree
>   of reverence that is due unto Thee...

Charles peeks. Sees Darrow look over at Mencken, who nods to the back. Darrow and Charles look back to see a sea of bowed heads.

Charles finds Rose again, bowed head. His face floods with shame.

Darrow makes a goofy face to Mencken, puts his finger to his lips and flibbers them like baby gibberish.

EXT. RHEA COUNTY COURTHOUSE LAWN

Out on the lawn 3,000 people listen over loudspeakers. There are picnic tables, picnic blankets populated by entire families. A large sign, "READ YOUR BIBLE" is tacked up on the side of the Courthouse.

The crowd is still and quiet. Men have taken off their hats. Joe Mendi the chimp takes his hat off too.

> REV. CARTWRIGHT (V.O.)
> Hear us in these, our prayers. And at the end of life's trouble, may we be admitted into the grace of Thy kingdom. And there, amongst the resplendent glories of a living God, offer praise to Thy glory and grace for evermore. Amen.

The crowd echoes "Amen" and the chimp chatters happily, waving his long arms over his head.

INT. RHEA COUNTY COURTHOUSE - DAY

Darrow and Neal sit with disgusted arms folded.

> DARROW
> I want it to be definitively noted that I objected to this prejudicial praying.

Judge Raulston clears his throat.

> JUDGE RAULSTON
> Duly noted, counsel.
>   (back to business)
> I'm calling the case of the State vs. John Thomas Scopes.
>   (to the prosecution)
> Mr. Attorney General, are you ready to proceed with the selection of the jury?

> HICKS
> Yes, sir.

The Bailiff goes over to a LITTLE GIRL (the one who gave radishes to Bryan) who sits up front and holds a bowler cap. Cameras flash.

In the crowd, Rose sees the girl and smiles affectionately.

The Bailiff picks out a name.

> BAILIFF
> J.P. Massingill.

JUMP CUT:

MASSINGILL sits on the stand being interviewed by the Judge.

          JUDGE RAULSTON
Mr. Massingill, do you know the defendant?

          MASSINGILL
Not more'n to nod.

          JUDGE RAULSTON
Could you go into the jury box and try the defendant wholly upon the law and the facts and render a fair and impartial verdict?

          MASSINGILL
I think so. Yes, sir.

          JUDGE RAULSTON
He seems to be competent, gentlemen. For the State?

McKenzie speaks up.

          MCKENZIE
No need, your honor. We know the juror and can vouch for his character.

Darrow raises his brow, "Is that a fact?" Judge Raulston looks at Darrow.

          JUDGE RAULSTON
Colonel Darrow?

Darrow approaches the stand more seriously. There is a long pause and the anticipation mounts. Finally...

          DARROW
Good morning.

          MASSINGILL
Good morning to you, sir.

          DARROW
What is your business, Mr. Massingill?

                    MASSINGILL

I am a minister.

                    DARROW

A minister?!

                    MASSINGILL

Yes, sir.

                    DARROW

Ever preach on evolution?

                    MASSINGILL

I haven't as a complete subject; I've taken it up in connection with other subjects.

                    DARROW

For it or against it?

                    MASSINGILL

I am strictly for the Bible.

                    DARROW

I'm sure you are, Reverend, but on the subject of evolution, did you preach for or against evolution?

                    MASSINGILL

I preached against it, of course!

Darrow dismissively waves his hand. The audience laughs, whoops, and applauds. Some stamp their feet. Judge Raulston bangs his gavel.

                    JUDGE RAULSTON

Quiet down! Quiet down!

INT. ADMINISTRATIVE OFFICE BELOW THE COURTHOUSE - DAY

TWO OFFICE LADIES look up as dust and a few plaster chips fall with the sound of stomping feet above them. The two look at each other, mouths agape.

INT. RHEA COURTHOUSE - DAY

Judge Raulston is now interviewing a new JUROR.

JUDGE RAULSTON
Could you go into the jury box and try the defendant wholly upon the law and the facts and render a fair and impartial verdict?

JUROR #1
I think so. Yes, sir.

A SERIES OF JUMP CUTS THROUGH ELEVEN OTHER JURORS, MEN OF VARIOUS AGES, YOUNG AND OLD, SITTING IN THE SAME CHAIR:

JUROR #2
Yes, sir, I can.

JUROR #3
Yep.

JUROR #4
Absolutely.

JUROR #5
Yes, I can.

JUROR #6
Uh huh.

JUROR #7
Sure will.

JUROR #8
Yes.

JUROR #9
Yes.

JUROR #10
Yes.

JUROR #11
Yes.

JUROR #12
No, sir.

Now Darrow stands before the last Juror, #12, not quite believing him.

> DARROW
> Now, Mr. Riley. You mean to tell me, you've never read anything about evolution at all?

> JUROR #12
> Well, no sir. I - I can't read.

This catches Darrow by surprise. Turns to his team.

> DARROW
> Oh! Well, I guess that means we have at least one honest juror in the bunch.

The defense team smiles in agreement.

OVER BY THE PROSECUTION

Bryan leans into Hicks.

> BRYAN
> I've never seen Darrow accept jurors so easily.

> HICKS
> Maybe he's planning on bribing them.

> JUDGE RAULSTON (O.S.)
> Recess for lunch.

INT. HALLWAY OUTSIDE THE COURTROOM - MOMENTS LATER

Mencken leads Charles through the throngs of exiting people. He pulls him aside in the hallway just outside the flow of traffic.

> MENCKEN
> Okay, tell me, what did you see?

Charles hesitates, unprepared, looking for something to say.

> CHARLES
> Jury selection?

> MENCKEN
> What - did - you - see?

Charles, flustered, gropes again.

CHARLES
A boring stretch of legal procedures.

MENCKEN
No no no no no. You saw a kangaroo court begin with a fundamentalist prayer cruelly condemning the accused before he's even been indicted.

Charles's eyes go wide. Oh yeeaaahh.

MENCKEN
Describe the two sides.

Charles thinks. Gets the idea.

CHARLES
Small town fundamentalists versus big city moderns?

MENCKEN
(not satisfied)
Eeeeehh. The defense: Highly competent, brilliant, eloquent, daring and patriotic. The prosecution: Bigots, ignorant, hatred, superstition, every sort of blackness that the human mind is capable of.

Now, Charles's eagerness drops a bit at what he's hearing.

MENCKEN
The judge, posturing before the yokels like a clown in a ten-cent sideshow. A courtroom swarming with rustic ignoramuses ready to lynch Scopes first chance they get.

CHARLES
Isn't it a little more -- complicated -- than that?

MENCKEN
Aim for simplicity, Mowgli, simplicity with punch. What did the jury consist of?

CHARLES
(referring to his notes)
Well, Six Baptists, four Methodists, one
Campbellite and one unaffiliated.

MENCKEN
Bible thumping half-wits and Holy Rollers. Visual
impressions, not "factual information."

CHARLES
But how do I separate fact from fiction?

MENCKEN
There are no facts, only interpretations.

Charles tries to take it all in, a bit overwhelmed, but trying hard.

EXT. RHEA COUNTY COURTHOUSE LAWN - DAY

Out on the courthouse lawn, a gospel group of four African-American men sing a beautiful Negro spiritual and the crowd is more integrated than one might expect.

Tables are filled with food for sale.

A group of children surround the chimp Joe Mendi. A little girl is mimicking Joe, making it difficult to discern which is the real monkey.

Rose sits with LeBarron under the shade of a tree with a plate of food.

INT. RHEA COUNTY COURTHOUSE — DAY

Rappleyea with Judge Raulston and the Bailiff pose for a picture, three proud little showmen with grinning teeth. FLASH!

The reporters swarm them for interviews. They're loving the attention.

INT. RHEA COUNTY COURTHOUSE — DAY

The crowd is back in their seats, sweating, wiping brows, fanning palm leaves.

Judge Raulston, sweating on his throne...

JUDGE RAULSTON
Bailiff, you may swear the jury in. That is, unless
the defense counsel would like to object to

swearing oaths before God, and every other legal
procedure in our country.

Darrow shakes his head no and waves him go ahead. He whispers to Neal and Malone.

>DARROW
>
>Moron.

The Bailiff holds the Bible up before the twelve men who raise their right hands.

>BAILIFF
>
>Do each of you, solemnly swear on the Holy Bible of Almighty God that you will diligently inquire into the truth and to well and truly try the issues. To find the facts without passion or prejudice, to apply the law without fear or favor?

>ALL THE JURORS
>
>I do.

>BAILIFF
>
>You may be seated.

They sit.

>JUDGE RAULSTON
>
>With the jury duly sworn, are we prepared now to hear the indictment?

>MCKENZIE
>
>Yes, your Honor.
>
>(reading)
>
>The grand jurors present that John T. Scopes did teach in the public schools, in violation of Tennessee law, and I quote: "a certain theory that denies the creation of man as taught in the Bible and did teach, instead, that man has descended from a lower order of animals," Close quote.

>JUDGE RAULSTON
>
>Gentlemen for the Defense?

NEAL
Your Honor, we would like to make a motion to dismiss the indictment at this time based on fourteen separate and sufficient grounds.

Judge Raulston looks eager for the show.

JUDGE RAULSTON
Proceed counsel.

INT. ADMINISTRATIVE OFFICE BELOW THE COURTROOM

Rappleyea is looking up at the plaster on the ceiling, worried. The two Office Ladies fret.

RAPPLEYEA
Has any more plaster fallen?

OFFICE LADY #1
No, sir. It's only when they stomp.

RAPPLEYEA
I'll call some engineers in. But until then, ladies, nothin' to nobody. Not even the Judge, capeesh?

The two ladies glance at each other and nod their heads.

INT. RHEA COUNTY COURTHOUSE - LATER

Darrow is in midstream presenting his conclusion...

DARROW
Your Honor, this is a foolish, mischievous, and wicked statute against all decency and learning!

The courtroom buzzes at this brazen insult.

Neal rolls his eyes. Malone prays for mercy.

Charles is shocked, Mencken smiles.

DARROW
Ignorance and fanaticism is all around us. If today you can make evolution a crime in the public school, tomorrow you can make it a crime in the

> private schools. Then you may ban books and newspapers. After a while, Your Honor, it is the setting of man against man and creed against creed until with flying banners and beating drums we are marching backward to the glorious ages of the sixteenth century when bigots burned men at the stake who dared to bring any intelligence and enlightenment and culture to the human mind.

Neal glares with anger. Malone hides his eyes.

Bryan shakes his head with amusement.

Darrow takes his seat. The crowd is split. Some applaud but others hiss and boo.

> JUDGE RAULSTON
> Order! Order!

Judge Raulston, heaves a heavy sigh. Ponders his due course.

> JUDGE RAULSTON
> My plan is to deliberate this evening over the Defense's motion to dismiss the indictment. I will present my verdict first thing Monday morning. Have a pleasant weekend. Court is adjourned.

The Judge's gavel raps.

INT. REPORTER WAREHOUSE - NIGHT

Twenty reporters are dictating to stenographers in rows. More stand in line. A GERMAN REPORTER dictates in German with English subtitles.

> GERMAN REPORTER
> ...The brilliant Darrow seems the only educated man in a room of ignorant fools...

A RUSSIAN REPORTER dictates in Russian with English subtitles.

> RUSSIAN REPORTER
> ...The United States has yet to abandon its religious superstition in order to build an advanced society, like that of the great Soviet state...

A FRENCH REPORTER dictates in French with English subtitles.

> FRENCH REPORTER
> ...The food here is terrible. They fry everything in grease...

Mencken, with Charles dutifully beside him, dictates to Rose from his notes, who is visibly annoyed at what she is hearing.

> MENCKEN
> Let no one mistake the trial for comedy, farcical though it may be in all its details. It serves notice on the country that Neanderthal man is organizing in these forlorn backwaters of the land, led by William Jennings Bryan, a fanatic, rid of sense and devoid of conscience...

INT./EXT. SCENES AROUND DAYTON

Various scenes show Daytonians and visitors alike generally enjoying the goings-on and acting decently, graciously -- helping women out of carriages, laughing over malts, smoking on a park bench, white and black teenagers tossing a ball, a family listening to a street quartet. People reading the papers, shocked Daytonians, sneering out-of-towners, and lastly, Rappleyea, who looks very distressed by what he reads.

> MENCKEN (V.O.)
> These Tennessee buffoons are the great masses of men. They are the mob at the dawn of history. They are ignorant, they are dishonest, they are cowardly, they are ignoble. They know little if anything that is worth knowing, and there is not the slightest sign of a natural desire among them to increase their knowledge.

INT./EXT. CHARLES'S AUTOMOBILE DRIVING - DAY

Charles drives an angry Rose along a scenic Tennessee route.

> ROSE
> That is not true, Charles! This is terrible! And then you reported to the whole world that Mr. Riley

can't read! He's a kind man. How could you write such things?

                CHARLES
Rose. It's the truth. He can't read.

                ROSE
It's selective truth. The things you don't say are just as important as the things you do.

Charles just sighs. He's not going to keep fighting. They pull up to the Sanitarium.

                ROSE
You gonna come in?

                CHARLES
I have to check the engine.

That bugs her, but she gets out and goes up to the front door. Charles watches her as he gets out and opens the car hood for a half-hearted engine inspection. There's obviously nothing wrong.

As Rose opens the door, Abigail jumps out to hug her. She's been waiting. Abigail waves whole-heartily to Charles. He gives a listless wave in return. Rose and Abigail go inside.

INT. SANITARIUM - DAY

A disinterested ORDERLY is there with them.

Abigail pulls a paper flower from behind her back and presents it to Rose with loving pride. It's a beautiful little thing, created out of construction paper, crayons and glue.

                ABIGAIL
Would you give this to Mr. Charles? I made it for him.

Rose smiles, trying hard to hold back tears.

Dr. Heydrich approaches Rose.

                DR. HEYDRICH
Rose, I need to speak to you alone.

INT. SANITARIUM CALMING WARD - DAY

Dr. Heydrich leads Rose through the calming ward. It's full of beds that look like flat horizontal cages with patients in them. Most are lying peacefully. But one of them lashes out like a wild animal trapped in a cage. Rose jumps.

>   DR. HEYDRICH
> Don't worry, they won't hurt you. We call it the
> "Utica crib." A new scientifically designed therapy
> from New York City. We use them for our more
> wild patients. It calms them down. Humanizes
> them.

Rose does not look convinced. They move on past a couple other patients sitting in straightjackets.

INT. DR. HEYDRICH'S OFFICE, SANITARIUM - DAY

Rose sits at Dr. Heydrich's desk. Dr. Heydrich sits down. He is unlike how Rose first met him. He is now detached, coldly scientific.

>   DR. HEYDRICH
> I'm afraid your sister has a tumor.

Rose's eyes go wide.

>   ROSE
> Oh my God.

>   DR. HEYDRICH
> But it's benign. And operable.
>   (hands over papers)
> If you sign these papers, we can take care of it next
> week. A specialist from Nashville is coming in.

Rose is overwhelmed with too much information.

>   ROSE
> It's benign?

>   DR. HEYDRICH
> Yes.

>   ROSE
> So that means she'll be okay?
>
>   DR. HEYDRICH
> She'll have to have a fallopian section, but yes, she'll be okay.
>
>   ROSE
> A what?
>
>   DR. HEYDRICH
> We'll have to remove her uterus.

Rose just sits there like all time has stopped. The weight of the world crashing down upon her.

>   ROSE
> She'll never be able to have children.
>
>   DR. HEYDRICH
> If we don't remove it, it may turn malignant.
>
>   ROSE
> I need a couple days to think about this.
>
>   DR. HEYDRICH
> Rose, it's really in your sister's best interest. We're only trying to do what's best for her -- and everyone.

Rose still stares in a daze.

INT. CHARLES'S AUTOMOBILE DRIVING - DAY

Charles and Rose drive back home.

>   CHARLES
> Like the doctor said, it's in Abbie's best interest.
>
>   ROSE
> But she hasn't complained about pain or anything.
>
>   CHARLES
> Rose, you're not a doctor. He knows what's best.

                    ROSE
I'm just not sure I trust him.

                    CHARLES
He's got a Ph.D. in medicine. He's a professional.
You're just a - just a...

                    ROSE
A what? A yokel?

Charles cringes like a puppy.

                    CHARLES
I'm sorry. I just meant that we don't know as
much as they do, that's all.

Rose looks off into the distance, thinking it all through. Charles turns optimistic.

                    CHARLES
I tell you what. Mr. Mencken's invited us back to
the night club. Why don't we just get away from it
all for the evening, have some fun, and maybe
you'll have a clearer mind in the morning.

Rose looks at him incredulously. Is he that dense?

                    ROSE
The Judge needed a stenographer tonight. I
volunteered.

Charles responds, crestfallen. They drive on in silence.

Charles looks over, sees Rose holding the paper flower.

                    CHARLES
What's that?

                    ROSE
It's a flower Abigail made. For you.

She hands it to him. Charles accepts it awkwardly.

                    CHARLES
Wow, that's great.

INT. JUDGE RAULSTON'S OFFICE AT THE COURTHOUSE - NIGHT

The Judge, pacing, finishes his dictation. Rose is at a portable stenographic machine typing his every word.

> JUDGE RAULSTON
> "...In view thereof, the Defense's motion to dismiss the case is hereby denied on all counts; the trial will, therefore, commence."

Rose looks up with interest. The Judge rips his notes once and tosses them into a basket. He looks sternly at Rose.

> JUDGE RAULSTON
> Young lady, it is of utmost importance that my decision remains in your strict confidence until I deliver it in court on Monday.

Rose nods earnestly.

INT. SPEAKEASY - NIGHT

Charles sits at a table with Mencken, a couple PARTYING MEN and a couple FLAPPERS. He's not getting into it. Mencken's on a roll.

> MENCKEN
> I drink exactly as much as I need. And a few drinks more.

More laughs. Mencken stops. Notices Charles's lack of participation.

> MENCKEN
> It appears Sampson here, is distraught over his Delilah.

Everyone gives Charles unwanted attention.

> MENCKEN
> You know what Nietzsche said about women? "In love woman is more barbaric than man. If you are going to have a woman, don't forget your whip."

Cheers from men, frowns from Flappers. Mencken pushes a beer toward Charles.

MENCKEN
Come on, Charles. Loosen up. Break a few laws.
You'll feel better in the morning.

Charles looks at Mencken, tired and broken down. Looks at the beer. Picks it up, and takes a swig. Everyone cheers. Mencken smiles with warm affection. They're starting to connect.

MENCKEN
So, where is she?

CHARLES
Transcribing for the Judge.

Mencken's eyes brighten with hunger.

MENCKEN
(leading)
So, your fiancé, knows the judge's decision on whether the trial will go on or not?

Charles stares at Mencken not following. Then it hits him.

CHARLES
No. No, I can't do that. I'm not going to use Rose to get a scoop.

Mencken's expression darkens.

MENCKEN
Well, what good is she to you, then?

CHARLES
There's got to be another way.

MENCKEN
You better think of one then, Mowgli. Your survival as a journalist depends on it.

Charles glares defiantly. He gets up to leave.

CHARLES
You'll have to excuse me, please.

And he leaves.

EXT. TENNESSEE MOUNTAINS - DAYBREAK

A beautiful sun breaks over the Tennessee mountains.

INT. DINING PORCH, AQUA HOTEL - DAY

Charles sits alone at a table, still bothered by last night, thinking it over.

Judge Raulston eats his breakfast alone at another table. He reads a newspaper editorial cartoon mocking the trial.

Charles watches the Judge from a distance. He's getting up the courage. But he also winces with a migraine. He knows what he has to do. He walks over to Raulston.

OVER BY RAULSTON

Charles approaches Raulston, rubbing his migraine.

> CHARLES
> Wonderful first day, your Honor.

> JUDGE RAULSTON
> Thank you, son. Enough to keep the papers selling, I trust.

> CHARLES
> More than enough, sir.

Raulston notices Charles wincing.

> JUDGE RAULSTON
> Burning the midnight oil?

> CHARLES
> (covering)
> Oh, uh, yeah. Reporter's job is never done.

Charles manages a weak smile. Raulston smiles knowingly.

> JUDGE RAULSTON
> Might wanna go easy on that oil.

Raulston places his napkin on the table. He's done.

                    JUDGE RAULSTON
Well, I have to apologize, but I don't have time for an interview. We're having some more photographs taken over at the courthouse.

                    CHARLES
Oh, all right then, sir. I can catch you later.

Raulston gets up and leaves. Charles calls after him.

                    CHARLES
Your honor! How about if I get the interview between your decision, and the next stage of the trial?

                    JUDGE RAULSTON
Sure. We'll have plenty of time in between.

                    CHARLES
See ya at church, tomorrow.

Raulston smiles, waves and continues on. Charles grins victoriously. The Judge has revealed more than he realizes. Charles looks over the room and sees Mencken finishing up his breakfast, watching him. Charles nods. Mencken grins.

EXT. BAPTIST CHURCH, DAYTON - DAY

The church's parking lot is full of cars and carriages. People crowd around exterior windows, looking in. It's overflowing.

INT. BAPTIST CHURCH, DAYTON - DAY

As the church sings the hymn, "Faith of Our Fathers," Charles looks around, uninvolved, next to Rose. He sees Judge Raulston sitting in the back pew next to Mrs. Bryan. Bryan sits up on the podium behind the song leader as the singing continues.

Charles looks over and sees the Bailiff, in street clothes, walk up behind the Judge and get his attention. The Judge looks perturbed. He gets up and exits the church.

EXT. BAPTIST CHURCH, DAYTON - DAY

The Bailiff hands the judge a copy of the Baltimore Sun with the headline, "MONKEY TRIAL WILL GO ON!" The Judge is livid.

INT. PRESS WAREHOUSE - DAY

Reporters are gathered around Rappleyea and Judge Raulston. Rappleyea is up front with Judge Raulston. An occasional clank comes from inside the open bathroom. Raulston thrusts forward the Sun paper.

> JUDGE RAULSTON
> Gentlemen, as I think I have made abundantly clear, I view this incident as a serious infraction. I will leave it to this august fraternity to determine who the "anonymous source" is that has breached the confidentiality of the Court.

> MENCKEN
> (furrowed brow, note pad in hand)
> Your Honor, how are you spelling "august"?

> JUDGE RAULSTON
> That's a-u-g . . .

Suddenly realizing his leg is being pulled, the Judge gathers his effects and disappears out the door. Rappleyea stands.

> RAPPLEYEA
> Men, I am going to make this short and sweet. Who did it?

There is only the shuffling of feet, nervous coughs, and clanking sounds from the bathroom. Several reporters glance at Mencken.

There is a flush. A PLUMBER sticks his head out of the toilet.

> PLUMBER
> Finally! Let the brown trout swim!

The reporters suppress smiles; Mencken jots down this line. Charles is sweating in his boots, looking around guiltily.

> RAPPLEYEA
> Nobody? Then it could only have been the stenographer. She'll have to be disciplined, of course.

Charles can take it no longer. He stands and clears his throat.

> CHARLES
> It wasn't the stenographer.

Mencken gives a look of shock at Charles.

> CHARLES
> It was me.

The Reporters buzz with excitement. Mencken grimaces. Then a bunch of them applaud. Charles is embarrassed by it all. Mencken watches him closely.

> CHARLES
> But I did not commit a breach of confidentiality.

INT. DINING PORCH, AQUA HOTEL - DAY

The Judge sits eating lunch with Rappleyea and Robinson.

> RAPPLEYEA
> He's a young man, your Honor. He stretched the rules, no doubt. But I could not tell you straight that he broke them. You yourself told him, in so many words, that the trial would continue.

> ROBINSON
> Of course he could then infer that you would deny the motion to dismiss.

> JUDGE RAULSTON
> I was tricked!

> RAPPLEYEA
> We hope, your Honor, that there can be some clemency on Charles's behalf.

                    (lowers his voice)
                And you know, we can't afford any more bad
                publicity than we're already gettin' from these big
                city papers.

The Judge's stern look softens.

EXT. FRONT PORCH, SMALL RESIDENCE - NIGHT

Charles knocks at the front door of a small residence. Rose opens and steps out on the porch.

                        CHARLES
                It's all been worked out, Rose. Everybody knows
                that you didn't reveal the Judge's opinion.

Rose slaps Charles across the cheek.

                        CHARLES
                What was that about!?

                        ROSE
                You tricked him. A hundred and fifty reporters in
                Dayton and you're the one who tricked the Judge.

                        CHARLES
                Aw, come on, Rose. It's just part of the job. I gotta
                get the story.

                        ROSE
                At the expense of honesty? Or have morals
                become just too "small town" for you?

                        CHARLES
                I've got to be creative. Adapt to the situation if I
                want to rise to the top.

                        ROSE
                The ends don't justify the means.

Charles is breaking. She's right and he knows it.

                        ROSE
                Did Mr. Mencken put you up to this?

                    CHARLES
          Actually, no. No, this was my idea.

                    ROSE
          Charles, you've changed since this whole thing
          started. It's like you're a different person.

He sighs.

                    CHARLES
          You're right. I think I just got caught up in the
          excitement of it all. -- No more shenanigans. The
          trial starts today. Straight shooting from here on out.
                    (heartfelt)
          I promise.

It takes a second before Rose, looking into his soul, can see that he's being genuine. A slight smile of approval crosses her lips.

                    CHARLES
          And speaking of promises.

Charles holds up a small ring box. And Rose's eyes go wide. She hugs him fiercely. All is forgiven.

INT. RHEA COUNTY COURTHOUSE - DAY

The courthouse is crowded again. Everyone already sweating and fanning themselves. Judge Raulston is mid-monologue.

                    JUDGE RAULSTON
          Now, as for the Defense's motion to dismiss, after
          careful consideration of the arguments, I have
          reached my decision. I am dismissing the motion
          and we will proceed with arguments forthwith.

The whole crowd bursts out in applause and whooping. More stomping too.

But not Darrow or Neal or Mencken. They look annoyed.

INT. BASEMENT, COURTHOUSE - DAY

The floor squeaks and creaks this time as more plaster falls.

EXT. RHEA COUNTY COURTHOUSE LAWN MID-MORNING

Out on the Courthouse lawn, two mothers fuss over their sons. MRS. MORGAN, mother of HOWARD MORGAN (14), smooths down a cowlick on Howard's head. Next to him, HARRY SHELDON (14).

> MRS. MORGAN
> Boys, we want you to sit tall in there. Make us proud.

> HOWARD
> I sure would hate to get Mr. Scopes in trouble.

> MRS. MORGAN
> You just tell the truth, Honey.

> OTHER STUDENT
> And Mr. Darrow just confuses me!

> OTHER MOTHER
> Mr. Darrow?

> HOWARD
> He wants us to remember all kinds of things that didn't happen!

> MRS. MORGAN
> (alarmed)
> When did you boys speak with Mr. Darrow?

INT. RHEA COUNTY COURTHOUSE MID-MORNING

Howard Morgan is on the stand. Hicks approaches.

> HICKS
> How old are you, Howard?

> MORGAN
> Fourteen.

> HICKS
> Did you study under Professor Scopes?

> MORGAN
> Yes, sir.

                    HICKS
Please state in your own words, Howard, just what it was he taught you.

                    MORGAN
Mr. Scopes said that the earth was once a hot molten mass. Then, when it cooled off a piece, there was a little germ formed. And this organism kept evolving until it got to be a pretty good-sized animal. Then it came on to be a land animal and kept on evolving. From this was man.

                                        CROSS DISSOLVE:

THE STAND - LATER

Darrow approaches the other kid, Harry.

                    HICKS
And how did Professor Scopes classify man with reference to the other animals?

                    HARRY
He said man had a reasoning power; that these other animals did not.

                    DARROW
Did he tell you what a mammal was? What makes man a mammal?

                    HARRY
Well... He taught why girls have bosoms. I remember that!

A great deal of laughter. Mrs. Morgan blushes.

Neal whispers to Malone.

                    NEAL
Now, that's education.

                    DARROW
Did Professor Scopes tell you anything else that was wicked?

> HARRY
> No, not as I remember of.

> DARROW
> Now, what he taught you, has it hurt you any?

> HARRY
> No, sir.

CROSS DISSOLVE:

INT. RHEA COUNTY COURTHOUSE - LATER

Darrow turns to Judge Raulston.

> DARROW
> Your Honor, we would like to call to the stand Dr. Maynard Metcalf, a Senior Professor at Johns Hopkins University.

Hicks hops to his feet.

> HICKS
> Your Honor, the State makes a motion to exclude as irrelevant the testimony of any scientist in this case.

At the defense table, Neal mutters to Malone and Scopes.

> NEAL
> Those weasels.
> (he hops up)
> This is ridiculous! We have to depose experts in order to prove that evolution does not contradict the Bible so the statute is not violated. Or should we just take a poll among the local hillbillies to decide?

The crowd murmurs. Now McKenzie pops up.

> MCKENZIE
> The Butler Act stipulates that teaching evolution contradicts the Bible. If you want to dispute that

claim, then change the law, don't try to change the meaning of words.

Raulston looks over at Bryan, who remains calm and silent.

> JUDGE RAULSTON
> I understand, Colonel Bryan, that you will be arguing for the Prosecution in favor of the motion to exclude expert testimony?

> BRYAN
> Yes, your honor.

> JUDGE RAULSTON
> I think it's time we hear from the Peerless Leader.

The crowd starts to applaud.

> JUDGE RAULSTON
> Stop that now!

They stop on cue.

Darrow and team look disgusted.

Judge Raulston looks at his pocket watch.

> JUDGE RAULSTON
> However, we'll have to wait to do so until after lunch.

He bangs the gavel. Everyone is up and moving. Mencken turns to see Charles already rushing out the door with Rose.

INT. SANITARIUM HALLWAY - DAY

The big Black Orderly casually leads Rose and Charles down a hallway.

> ORDERLY
> Miss Abigail gonna be all right?

Rose gives a curious look. How did he know?

> ROSE
> Yes. She's having fallopian surgery.

CHARLES
He doesn't know what that is.

ORDERLY
No mo' babies.

Charles and Rose look at each other as they continue on.

ORDERLY
No mo' babies for Miss Abigail and de othas.

Rose can't believe her ears. Neither can Charles.

INT. DR. HEYDRICH'S OFFICE - DAY

Dr. Heydrich sits staring in emotionless silence at his desk. He has been asked a question and is considering how to answer it. It's an uncomfortable silence. And his response is dry, scientific.

DR. HEYDRICH
The problem is that so few people understand eugenics. So, we explain it in terms they can understand.

ROSE
You lied to me, doctor. You said she had a tumor.

DR. HEYDRICH
You have to realize, Miss Williams, when the weak members of society propagate their own kind, the health of the entire race is in jeopardy. The procedure is simply a scientific means of weeding out the unfit.

Rose and Charles's mouths are agape.

CHARLES
By sterilizing her?

ROSE
You can't do this. This is illegal.

> DR. HEYDRICH
> I'm afraid it's not. In fact, twenty five states already have sterilization laws.

> ROSE
> I'll bring her to another asylum.

> DR. HEYDRICH
> Where? Bolivar? Knoxville? They all have the same policy we do. In fact, a majority of the medical community in America is in virtual agreement on the need for eugenics. Are you so presumptuous as to defy the whole of modern medicine, Miss Williams?

Rose doesn't know how to respond, so Charles jumps in to help.

> CHARLES
> But you still need Rose's signature.

> DR. HEYDRICH
> Yes. The procedure is not compulsory yet.

Rose gets up to leave.

> ROSE
> Well, then I'm taking Abigail out of here. Let's go, Charles.

> DR. HEYDRICH
> I'm afraid you can't do that.

They stop. Heydrich pushes a secret button under his table.

> DR. HEYDRICH
> You see, Abigail's admittance papers, that you signed, stipulate that she cannot be released unless she is sterilized.

Rose is in shock.

> DR. HEYDRICH
> So, either way, Abigail is going to have to have the operation. If you sign the papers now, we can get

>   this over with in a couple days, and you can do
>   whatever you please with her.
>
>   ROSE
>   She's not some animal that we "do what we please
>   with."

Just then, the door opens and TWO HUGE ORDERLIES enter.

Charles looks up at them. Do not fool with these dogs.

>   DR. HEYDRICH
>   Please do consider signing the papers, Miss
>   Williams. We have two more days left. It's for the
>   greatest good.

INT. CHARLES'S AUTOMOBILE DRIVING - DAY

Charles speeds back to the court. Rose cannot contain her crying. Charles surreptitiously looks at his pocket watch.

INT. RHEA COUNTY COURTHOUSE - DAY

The court is in session. Rose sits in her spot in the crowd, still wiping her wet eyes. Charles watches her with sympathy, but Mencken pokes him and gets his attention back up front.

Bryan moves to the front of the courtroom.

>   BRYAN
>   If the Court please, until now I have not thought it
>   fit to take part in this trial. Of course, I have
>   frequently entered the case by reference. For the
>   sin of opposing evolution, my wife informs me
>   that I have been personally insulted by members
>   of the Defense 29 times thus far -- and twice by the
>   monkey outside.

Laughter fills the court.

>   BRYAN
>   Now, Professor Scopes taught that man has
>   evolved from lower forms of life. This is the

undisputed fact in evidence. So why now the need for experts? I will tell you why. Diversion.

He grabs a book off the prosecution table.

> BRYAN
> In this school textbook - A Civic Biology by George W. Hunter - one of their "experts" - we are told that man is no different from all the other mammals. No different at all. Talk about putting Daniel in the lion's den!

Laughter and applause. Mencken rolls his eyes.

> BRYAN
> They've supplanted the Bible and its Golden Rule "Do unto others" with a new standard of morality: survival of the fittest. Where the weak are considered unfit and eliminated by the strong.

Bryan looks over at his wife, poignantly in her wheelchair.

Bryan holds the book up.

> BRYAN
> Read it, friends! It's here in the Biology textbook that little Howard Morgan has been given by the "experts" to learn and to live by! It is this doctrine, your Honor, this ethic of animal supremacy, held by their experts, that further gave us the military machine in Germany and their hero, Nietzsche.
> (points to Darrow)
> Why, we have the testimony of my friend here from Chicago in the Leopold and Loeb murder case just last year...

> DARROW
> Objection, your Honor! I know where this is going!

> JUDGE RAULSTON
> Objection overruled.

EXT. LARGE CULVERT - DAY

Dreamlike memory sequence: A drainage ditch under a bridge. Two teenaged boys, the cherubic innocent ones defended by Darrow in the first scene, but now vicious and strident, subdue and stab a third teenaged boy in a brutal, blurred, slow motion murder. Their faces then appear as shown in the earlier courtroom scene standing behind Darrow.

BRYAN (V.O.)
Leopold and Loeb, the wealthy Chicago teenagers who murdered a neighbor-boy in cold blood, read Nietzsche extensively and had adopted his philosophy of the supermen: Those who believe they are beyond good and evil. Above the laws of common men.

The boys laugh deliriously at their mayhem, wiping blood off their hands and clothes.

BRYAN (V.O.)
And we have Mr. Darrow's argument in court -- that his client was not responsible for the murder, but that the theory of evolution was.

INT. RHEA COUNTY COURTHOUSE - DAY

Back to the present. Darrow is furious.

DARROW
I object to an injection of that case into this one! It is prejudice!

JUDGE RAULSTON
Overruled.

Bryan points at little Howard and Harry.

BRYAN
Now, my friends, Mr. Darrow asked these young boys, "Did the teaching of evolution do you any harm?" Why did he not ask the victim of Leopold and Loeb?

Darrow glares malignantly at Bryan.

INT. PRESS WAREHOUSE - NIGHT

Charles enters the press warehouse. Reporters sit talking in various groups or lie alone, flat on their cots reading or writing. The mood is downcast as if their man has just lost the case. Charles brings a book in his hands.

                CHARLES
Have any of y'all seen this book? The one Mr. Bryan quoted. Hunter's Biology.

Reporters listen up. Some draw near in interest.

                CHARLES
It says on page 196 that white people are a higher race than the Negro, and the Asian and the Indian.

Eyes go wide. One of the Chinese reporters steps in. Grabs the book.

             CHINESE REPORTER
Let me see that.

A few more reporters come near. Charles grabs it back. Reads it.

                CHARLES
Look at this. On page 263 it says the feebleminded, epileptics and handicapped "are parasites upon the race. If such people were lower animals, we would probably kill them off to prevent them from spreading."

The two German reporters from an earlier scene turn and glance at each other. The others are horrified.

                CHARLES
Mr. Bryan is right. They're teaching this to the kids. In every school in the country.

Suddenly, Mencken materializes out of the crowd. Steps up to Charles. Takes the book. Carefully closes it without looking at it.

MENCKEN
I don't know about this book, but I do know what I saw in court today. And that's the story I'm here to cover. I saw a bitter, impotent, washed-up politician argue with a straight face that the barbarian hordes are better suited to determine the curriculum of the Tennessee public schools than expert scientists.

The group is silent. Some begin to nod in agreement. Charles listens with shock on his face.

MENCKEN
I saw a tin-pot fundamentalist Pope, claim that man was not a mammal.

EXT. STREETS OF DAYTON - SUNSET

The sun is setting. Mencken and Charles walk, winding their way to the edge of town and then down a dirt road as they talk.

CHARLES
I don't necessarily disagree, Mr. Mencken. It's just that you seem to exaggerate in one direction, yet completely ignore counter evidence.

MENCKEN
Such as?

CHARLES
Such as the content of that book, for instance, and how they're tryin' to sterilize certain people, right here in Tennessee, based on its theories.

MENCKEN
It's irrelevant to the case.

CHARLES
Did you know John Scopes never taught evolution? That's why the defense won't let him take the stand. Because it might invalidate the trial. Those two kids, they were coached by

Darrow on what to say. It wasn't even true. I also looked into Mr. Darrow's background.

Mencken looks surprised.

CHARLES
Turns out he was indicted in the past for jury tampering, bribery, breaking the law for the sake of his "cause." How come no one's reporting those facts?

Mencken snaps.

MENCKEN
Charles!

Charles stops dead. Mencken, regains his composure, lights a cigar.

MENCKEN
Charles, we select facts in our profession because we have no alternative. We have deadlines, column inches, audience demands. But at the end of the day, why are we journalists? Hmmm? Why?

CHARLES
To discover truth?

MENCKEN
To change the world. Is that all you want to do is "discover the truth" or do you want to create truth? Build a new world, free from the fetters of fundamentalism.

The two now stand by a desolate lot, the edge of a cemetery. Charles looks upset. Mencken leads him through the cemetery.

MENCKEN
Let me tell you a story of two men. Both started out side-by-side -- both young, both wanting to be journalists. One of them wanted to use his words to change the world, even if the majority of inferiors hated him for it. His success increased.

> He became, in time, the most influential columnist in America.

Charles looks up at Mencken. He can tell Mencken is talking about himself.

> MENCKEN
> Some said he stretched the truth. But if he did, he had good reason. A higher cause. The cause, he learned, is more important than any particular detail. That cause is the truth.

There is a moment of silence. Mencken takes a puff.

> CHARLES
> And the other reporter?

> MENCKEN
> He wanted to discover the truth, wherever it led him. He let others control him. Others' rules, others' religion. He never made it in the big city. He started a useless little local paper in an out of the way town nobody cares about. He died in obscurity and insignificance.

Mencken drops his cigar. He steps it into the ground. The two are standing above a gravestone in a cemetery. The gravestone reads, "William Anderson 1858 - 1921."

> CHARLES
> (whispers to himself)
> My father.

> MENCKEN
> You've got the talent, kid. Don't squander it on the grave of puritan virtue.

Charles's eyes well up looking at his father's grave. He looks up, and Mencken is gone. Like he disappeared. Charles looks back at the grave, the dark night of his soul.

INT. PRESS WAREHOUSE, STENO-POOL - NIGHT

The line of stenos and reporters dictating. Rose sits, poised at her stenographic machine. Charles, a new man, sits with her and begins to dictate from his notes.

> CHARLES
> In court today, the audience was more than a little amused as the confused and befuddled William Jennings Bryan denied that he was a mammal.

Rose stops typing, but Charles doesn't notice. He continues.

> CHARLES
> All a desperate plea to protect fundamentalism from the knowledge of science and experts.

Charles stops. Realizes Rose has stopped. She's staring at him.

> CHARLES
> What?

> ROSE
> Charles, I was there. He did not deny he was a mammal. And he was not "desperate." He was rather self-confident, actually.

> CHARLES
> It's making a point, Rose, now please?

He gestures to keep typing. Rose doesn't move.

> ROSE
> But it isn't true.

> CHARLES
> It's my opinion, okay?

> ROSE
> Is it? Or is it Mr. Mencken's?

> CHARLES
> I can think for myself, thank you.

                    ROSE
    Mr. Bryan made a knowledgeable argument. Why
    would you try to make him look like an
    uneducated bigot?

                    CHARLES
    Because maybe that's what I think he is.
        (let's it sink into her)
    That's right, Rose. Maybe I don't think evolution is
    all that bad for kids. Maybe I think
    fundamentalists like Bryan are responsible for this
    plague of puritanism, stupidity and buncombe!

Rose stares at him in realization. A moment of awkward silence.

Then she takes her engagement ring off her finger...

                    ROSE
    Well, if that's how you feel, then I think we've
    made a mistake.

She hands the ring back to him. He stares in shock. Rose gathers her purse to leave. He calls after her.

                    CHARLES
    You're going to break our engagement because of
    my opinion of Bryan?

Rose turns back.

                    ROSE
    No, Charles. It's because you've changed. You've
    become a man who's willing to lie in order to
    achieve your ambition. A man whose personal
    agenda is more important than the truth. And
    that's a man I can't respect.

Now Charles starts to break out.

                    CHARLES
    You're so caught up in the details, you can't even
    see the higher cause. You're a slave to this small

> town. It's rules, it's religion. I think you're just afraid of progress.

>> ROSE
>> You're right. I am afraid of progress. Progress that wants to sterilize my sister in the name of science and the "good of society."

Charles is stunned into silence.

>> ROSE
>> I remember you told me you were afraid of becoming your father. Well, you don't have to worry about that, Charles. He wouldn't have done this.

Rose tramples out, leaving Charles alone. He gestures with frustration at his outburst.

And suddenly, he notices, all the typing has stopped and everyone has been listening to them. His face turns beet red.

From a shadowy area in the corner, Mencken observes unnoticed.

INT. RHEA COUNTY COURTHOUSE - DAY

The courtroom is packed. Sweaty. Palm leaf fans, waving.

Charles sits with Mencken. He glances behind him. Rose is not there.

Malone addresses the Judge.

>> MALONE
>> ...The truth does not need guards at the gate, your Honor. It just needs the gate to be open. The truth always wins and we are not afraid of it. The truth is no coward. We ask, therefore, your Honor, to open wide the gates of knowledge to the students of Tennessee and to permit the admission of scientific experts as a matter of correct law, as a matter of sound procedure, and as a matter of simple justice!

The audience bursts into extended applause. Many begin standing. Darrow looks behind him in surprise. Mumbles to Malone.

> DARROW
> What the hell are they clapper-clawing for? He's on our side.

> MALONE
> Maybe they aren't as bigoted as we think.

Darrow waves it away.

In the midst of the clamor the Bailiff is rapping his nightstick on a table, banging out his approval. To Rappleyea's horror, people stamp their feet. He looks at the floor waiting any moment for it to collapse.

INT. ADMINISTRATIVE OFFICE BELOW THE COURTHOUSE

A heavy shower of plaster falls from the office ceiling. TWO CONSTRUCTION ENGINEERS lead a work team of men in setting up a couple of makeshift wooden support pylons under the joists. They all stop when they hear one of the main cross beams make a distinctly loud cracking sound. They fall off their ladders and back away, expecting it to crush them. But it doesn't.

> INT. COURTROOM
> Judge Raulston at his bench.

> JUDGE RAULSTON
> Tomorrow, I'll rule on whether expert testimony will be admitted to this case.

The gavel hits the pad.

INT. COURTROOM - MINUTES LATER

The courtroom is clearing of everyone. Scopes, Malone and Bryan pack up their things. The others are already on their way out.

Charles comes back into the room for his pad. He finds it, just in time to notice Bryan respectfully approaching Malone.

> BRYAN
> Dudley, that was the finest speech on any subject I have ever heard.

                    MALONE
          I only regret that it had to be delivered in
          opposition to you, Chief.

                    BRYAN
               (thoughtfully)
          The truth has nothing to fear all right.

                    MALONE
          William. I respect your concern for the rights of
          the majority. But what if one day, the tables are
          turned, and it's your view that is in the minority?

Charles sees Bryan nod thoughtfully in response.

EXT. STREET OUTSIDE COURTHOUSE - DAY

As the masses of people leave the courthouse, limping Snakehead and his buddies sneer as they watch Bryan leave the building.

In the street, a fancy out-of-town automobile pulls up to the curb. Everybody notices.

And then THREE MEN step out. They're dressed to the "T" in pinstripe suits, long coats and hats. Very upscale, and very out of place in this country world. They scan the crowds looking for someone as the crowd stares back, whispering among themselves of gangsters and hoodlums.

Up on the courthouse steps, Rappleyea is exiting. He sees the New York men scanning the crowd. With a worried look, he dodges out of sight back into the building.

INT./EXT. CHARLES'S AUTOMOBILE - DAY

Charles pulls up to the Mansion with Mencken in the passenger seat. They're silent for a second as Mencken thinks about what to say.

                    MENCKEN
          You did the right thing, Mowgli. Women aren't
          used to dealing with the larger riddles of life.
          Which makes them essentially petty.

Charles nods but isn't looking entirely convinced.

MENCKEN
All right. When we go inside, I don't want you saying a thing. Just shut up and listen.

INT. THE MANSION - DAY

Darrow, Malone and Neal are with six scientists. Mencken and Charles sit to the side, more observers than participants.

DARROW
Worried? About what?!

SCIENTIST #1
We have no problem testifying as scientific experts on evolution, but...

He looks at his fellow scientists.

DARROW
But what?!

SCIENTIST #1
What if he asks us about our medical affiliations?

DARROW
What medical affiliations?

The scientists get a bit uncomfortable.

SCIENTIST #2
Most of us are on boards of eugenic societies.

Malone and Neal both react with discouragement.

NEAL
Oh, for god's sake. Bryan will have a field day with that one. Conspiracy theories and mass hysteria.

DARROW
I can just see the old blowhard wheeling his wife up to the front of the court and asking if they want to sterilize her.

The scientists don't look too sure of themselves.

Charles takes positive note of that.

Darrow decides his course.

> DARROW
> You must not go on the stand.

Everyone looks at Darrow with unbelief.

> DARROW
> We have to find a way to get your testimonies into the record without allowing Bryan to cross examine you.

Charles shows a growing concern that he hides from Mencken.

EXT. DAYTON LIBRARY - NIGHT

Charles enters the Dayton public library.

INT. DAYTON LIBRARY - NIGHT

Charles sits at a table, alone in the little place, with a pile of books spread out on the table before him. He looks at the cover of a magazine, BIRTH CONTROL REVIEW. Opens it. Reads. The Voice-overs we hear are various writers and authorities...

> FEMALE VOICE (V.O.)
> There is but one practical program in handling the feeble-minded, the mentally defective and the moron: Sterilization.

He turns the page, reads...

INT. DR. HEYDRICH'S OFFICE - NIGHT

The voice-over continues over a scene of Rose sadly signing release papers in Dr. Heydrich's presence. She has no other choice to get her sister out...

> MALE VOICE (V.O)
> The hordes of degenerates, diseased, idiotic, and feeble minded, must be wiped out.

He opens another book...

MALE VOICE (V.O.)
It is our duty to eliminate all abnormal and parasitical members of society."

INT. DAYTON LIBRARY - NIGHT

As Charles turns another book page and reads...

FEMALE VOICE (V.O.)
Eugenics is the most adequate solution to racial, political and social problems.

Charles shuts the book, deeply disturbed by what he has read.

EXT. DARK WOODS - NIGHT

From a distance, a great bonfire can be seen through the thicket of a deep woods. Mysterious shadows of a group of people.

EXT. BONFIRE IN THE WOODS - NIGHT

Men in white sheets. Burning cross. A Ku Klux Klan gathering. About twenty men glaring up at their work of art. The IMPERIAL DRAGON pulls one of the cloaked members aside.

The Dragon hands the member a photograph.

It's a picture of William Jennings Bryan. The faceless soldier nods -- and limps away, with the distinct limp of Snakehead.

INT. HALLWAY OUTSIDE THE COURTROOM - DAY

Rappleyea walks briskly down the hallway toward the courtroom. He's late. Court's in session.

Suddenly, hands come out and jerk him down a side hallway. Slam him up against the wall.

It's the Three New York Gangsters. They look on him like a trio of soulless sharks smelling blood. But then, the Gangster who pulled him in, releases his grip and smooths out Rappleyea's jacket. Don't want it all rustled.

RAPPLEYEA
Hey, fellas. What brings you here?

                         LEAD GANGSTER
            Rapp. You haven't contacted your creditors, and
            you're late on your first payment.

                         RAPPLEYEA
            That property is going to move, you watch. I've
            got several inquiries already.

The Lead Gangster eyes him suspiciously.

                         LEAD GANGSTER
            The papers don't make it sound too good.

                         RAPPLEYEA
                     (nervous laughter)
            Bad publicity is still publicity.

The two support Gangsters look at each other confused.

                         RAPPLEYEA
            Look, I'm workin' on it, fellas. Day and night. I
            should have a deal signed by the end of the week.

The Lead Gangster looks at the others. They shrug. Sure. He turns back to Rappleyea. humiliatingly waves him on.

                         LEAD GANGSTER
            You got a week. Don't make a monkey outta me.

The Lead Gangster looks at the other two for approval.

                         LEAD GANGSTER
            Get it? Monkey.

They look at each other and chuckle.

                         GANGSTER #2
            Yeah, monkey.

Rappleyea laughs nervously and crawls away like a scared rat.

INT. RHEA COUNTY COURTHOUSE AFTERNOON

Rappleyea enters the courtroom, fixing his tie. Inside the courtroom the Judge is winding up his ruling.

JUDGE RAULSTON
...the Court concludes that expert testimony would shed no light on the factual issues relevant to the case at bar. The motion to exclude scientific testimony, therefore, is hereby sustained; the scientific experts for the Defense will not be permitted to testify.

The crowd murmurs with interest. Darrow stands.

DARROW
What about scientific testimony offered with the jury not present?

JUDGE RAULSTON
Why?

DARROW
We need to create a record for the appellate court's review.

JUDGE RAULSTON
You assumin' defeat, Colonel?

DARROW
No, your honor. But considering the environment, I'm just being realistic.

BRYAN
And I presume we will be entitled to cross-examine their scientists?

DARROW
Absolutely not!

JUDGE RAULSTON
Why not?

DARROW
Not testimony offered merely for appellate review!

JUDGE RAULSTON
Well now, Colonel, wouldn't it help ascertain the truth in this trial?

DARROW
Has there been any effort to ascertain the truth in this trial?

The crowd murmurs. A hiss or two can be heard. One man pipes up rather loudly, angrily, "Hey!" Malone looks down.

HICKS
Objection!

DARROW
(exasperated)
Oh, forget about the live testimonies, your Honor. We'll just submit written affidavits -- for the prospective benefit of those who dare to think!

Judge Raulston reacts with shock at the insult. More murmuring in the crowd. Darrow turns, winks and smiles at Malone and Neal. They mutter to each other.

NEAL
It worked.

MALONE
Brilliant.

The prosecution is dumbfounded. Bryan whispers to Hicks.

BRYAN
That's one-sided testimony. When do we get to tell our side?

HICKS
Your closing speech to the jury. You'll get your chance, Mr. Bryan.

Over by the press, Mencken smirks. Charles listens intently.

The Judge brings them back into the trial.

JUDGE RAULSTON
I hope, Colonel, that you do not mean to reflect upon the Court with that accusation.

Darrow turns acidly sarcastic.

DARROW
Well, your Honor certainly has the right to hope.

The Judge's eyes burn with insult.

JUDGE RAULSTON
I have the right to do something else as well! I'm citing you, Colonel, for contempt of Court.

Judge Raulston bangs his gavel. Darrow looks shocked.

The Prosecution table looks up. The Crowd murmurs.

JUDGE RAULSTON
You have unlawfully impugned the good name of this state and the dignity of this court. You will appear before me two weeks from today to answer this charge.

The crowd continues murmuring. The cameras flashing. Reporters scribbling. Charles is one of them.

Darrow considers his crime. Sighs deeply. The crowd starts to calm down. Darrow turns back to the judge.

DARROW
I'm sorry, your honor. I apologize to the court for such hasty remarks.

And the entire courtroom goes completely silent.

Reporters stop scribbling. Charles is all ears. Mencken frowns.

Bryan and company are in shock.

Even the judge raises his brow in surprise.

Darrow has his head bowed in thoughtful shame. And then he says with the most sincerity he has spoken the entire trial.

>   DARROW
> I have not found upon any citizen here in this
> town, the slightest discourtesy. I have been treated
> better, kindlier and more hospitably than I would
> have been up north. And that is due largely to the
> hospitality of the southern people. Although I did
> not intend contempt, I should not have made the
> remark, and I am sorry.

A moment more of dead silence.

And then the entire courthouse bursts out in applause.

Even Bryan and the prosecution.

Even the Judge.

But not Mencken, who rolls his eyes.

The crowd quiets down and Judge Raulston speaks up, with a tear in his eye. He is genuinely touched.

>   JUDGE RAULSTON
> Colonel Darrow, the man that I believe died on the
> cross to save us from sin, taught that it was godly
> to forgive. I believe in that man -- and I accept
> your apology.

More applause and cheers.

Darrow sits down next to Neal and Malone. Neal mutters under his breath.

>   NEAL
> Regular Valentino.

>   DARROW
> I had you going. Don't deny it.

But Malone looks at the crowd sympathetically.

EXT. RHEA COUNTY COURTHOUSE - DAY

Time has passed. The crowds are leaving the courthouse.

INT. RHEA COUNTY COURTHOUSE - DAY

Charles is leaving with Mencken. He stops when he notices Rose making her way to the front.

Judge Raulston is gathering his things to leave. Rose reaches him.

> ROSE
> Excuse, me Judge.

> JUDGE RAULSTON
> Yes, young lady, how can I help you?

> ROSE
> May I ask you some legal questions?

> JUDGE RAULSTON
> I'm on the way to my office. Why don't you follow me there?

INT. JUDGE RAULSTON'S OFFICE - DAY

Judge Raulston sits at his desk with a tearful Rose looking to him.

> JUDGE RAULSTON
> I'm afraid there's not much you can do, Rose. You signed the papers. It's all legal.

Rose is unmoved. The Judge searches for another answer.

> JUDGE RAULSTON
> I could sign a temporary restraining order on the asylum.

Rose lights up with hope.

> JUDGE RAULSTON
> But that would require an attorney to file the appropriate papers. Take a few days.

> ROSE
> I can't afford an attorney. And I don't have a few days.

> JUDGE RAULSTON
> I'm sorry, Rose.

Rose breaks down in tears. Judge awkwardly pats her for comfort. He doesn't know women very well.

INT. COURTHOUSE BASEMENT - DAY

Rappleyea is overseeing the Construction Engineers place the wooden support pylons in place under the cross beams on the ceiling. One of the Engineers is looking at a newspaper with him. It's a big headline, with a big editorial cartoon making a monkey out of Rappleyea.

> RAPPLEYEA
> Now, listen fellas, nobody, and I mean nobody is
> to know about this little patch up job, you hear?

The construction men grunt approval.

The Engineer next to him points to the cartoon and laughs annoyingly. Rappleyea gives him a dirty look, and the guy straightens out and gets back to work.

> RAPPLEYEA
> We've already got enough negative press to choke
> a gorilla. I can't afford to lose any more audience.

INT. COURTHOUSE BASEMENT OFFICES - DAY

Judge Raulston exits his office. He stops. Hears some pounding noise. He walks curiously toward a door. Hears more sounds. Opens the door.

INT. COURTHOUSE BASEMENT - DAY

Rappleyea and the men all stop dead and look at the Judge with open mouths.

> RAPPLEYEA
> Hey, Judge.

> JUDGE RAULSTON
> We got us some structural problems here?

Rappleyea deflates and confesses like a kid with his hand caught in the cookie jar.

                    RAPPLEYEA
          I didn't want anyone to panic. But I gotta be
          honest, your honor, we might have to cut the
          attendance down -- if we want to keep the floor
          from caving in.

                    JUDGE RAULSTON
          And lose all those customers for Dayton
          commerce? Are you kidding, George?

Rappleyea brightens up. Raulston thinks a moment.

                    JUDGE RAULSTON
          I got a better idea.

EXT. COURTHOUSE LAWN - DAY

The Judge sits on the platform at the front of the Courthouse lawn. 2,000 people surround the stage. Some in the shade of trees, most under the hot sun. Large speakers so they can all hear.

Rappleyea is in the audience smiling, proud. He looks over and sees the three Gangsters smile at him, and his smile melts.

Rose is there with LeBarron. She looks and sees Charles with Mencken up by the press area.

                    JUDGE RAULSTON
          Well, counsel, does that complete your reading
          into the record of expert testimony?

                    NEAL
          Yes, your honor. We're pleased.

                    JUDGE RAULSTON
          Why don't we adjourn until tomorrow, then?

Defense and Prosecution start packing up.

Darrow stands up.

                    DARROW
          Your Honor. There is one more thing.

This surprises even Neal and Malone.

> JUDGE RAULSTON
> And what might that be, Colonel?

> DARROW
> The Defense would like to call Mr. William Jennings Bryan to the stand.

Mencken and Charles look surprised.

The Prosecution looks surprised.

Even the defense looks surprised.

And yes, the Judge as well.

> JUDGE RAULSTON
> Colonel Bryan?

> DARROW
> As an expert witness on the Bible.

A loud murmur breaks out. The crowd is finally surprised.

At the Prosecution table, Hicks leans back in his chair with amusement. Bryan sits forward with intrigue.

> JUDGE RAULSTON
> Now let me get this right, Colonel. You want to call a lawyer from the other side to testify against your client?

> DARROW
> Yes, your honor.

Judge Raulston has to think about that one a moment.

OVER BY THE PROSECUTION TABLE

Bryan, Hicks and McKenzie are huddled for strategy.

> MCKENZIE
> It's never been done!

> HICKS
> Leave it to that old fox.

OVER BY THE DEFENSE

Malone and Neal are just as distressed as the Prosecution.

> NEAL
> What the hell are you doing?

> MALONE
> This is what you were here for all along, isn't it?

> DARROW
> (grinning deviously)
> It was your idea.

> JUDGE RAULSTON (O.S.)
> Well, I see no reason to deny. Prosecution?

OVER BY THE PROSECUTION

> HICKS
> May we have a moment, your Honor?

By the time he pops back to the team, Bryan is decided.

> BRYAN
> I'll do it.

> HICKS
> This is not a debate, Mr. Bryan! This is a cross-examination with the Devil.

> MCKENZIE
> He cheats for breakfast and lies for lunch.

> BRYAN
> I'm not afraid of him.

OVER BY THE DEFENSE

> DARROW
> I'll have complete control.

> NEAL
> (wising up)
> He'll be walking into a trap.

OVER BY THE PROSECUTION

> HICKS
> You'll be walking into a trap. If you go up on that stand, you can only lose.

> MCKENZIE
> Jesus would lose.

That makes Bryan think. But before they can marshal any more arguments, Bryan is up and addressing the court.

> BRYAN
> If your honor please, I insist in advance that if I take the stand, then Mr. Darrow can be put on the stand for his views.

This suggestion further delights the crowd and the Judge. Raulston looks to Darrow for approval. Darrow shrugs, "why not?"

OVER BY THE DEFENSE

Malone jerks Darrow down to the table.

> NEAL
> You can't go on that stand.

> MALONE
> He'll carve you up just as bad.

> DARROW
> If I ever make it to the stand.

Darrow winks. Neal and Malone start to get it. Darrow stands up.

> DARROW
> Yes, your Honor, we agree to the terms.

OVER BY CHARLES AND MENCKEN

Charles looks around. Whispers to Mencken.

> CHARLES
> Where's Scopes?

                    MENCKEN
          Scopes who? This is what this trial is all about,
          Mowgli. Scopes was an appetizer.

THE SUN UP IN THE SKY

Exposes all to its burning rays. Everything is out in the open.

OUT ON THE STREET AT A DISTANCE

A beat up farm truck drives slowly by the crowd. It's driven by Snakehead. In the front seat is a rifle and the photo of Bryan he received from the Grand Dragon. He looks at the outside court with contempt. Spits out the window.

EXT. COURTHOUSE LAWN - DAY

Bryan is on the stand. Darrow paces as he questions. Behind the stand on the courthouse wall is a huge sign: "READ YOUR BIBLE."

                    DARROW
          You have given considerable study to the Bible
          haven't you, Mr. Bryan?

                    BRYAN
          Yes, sir; I have tried to.

                    DARROW
          You have written articles and sometimes made
          interpretations of various things?

Neal and Malone look at each other. Good trap.

                    BRYAN
          I would say comments on the lessons.

                    DARROW
          And in these lessons do you claim that everything
          in the Bible should be literally interpreted?

                    BRYAN
          I believe everything should be taken as it is given
          there. Certainly some of the Bible is illustrative.
          For instance, "Ye are the salt of the earth," is not
          intended to mean that man is literally salt.

                    DARROW
    But when you read that the whale swallowed
    Jonah, how do you interpret that?

                    BRYAN
    I believe it. I believe in a God who can make a
    whale and can make a man and make both do as
    He pleases.

                    DARROW
    You figure it was a fish off the shelf, or one made
    for just that purpose?

                    BRYAN
    You may guess; you evolutionists are fond of
    guessing.

Laughter in the crowd. Even Mencken smirks. Touché. Mencken looks disapprovingly at Charles busily taking notes.

                    MENCKEN
    Devil's in the details, Mowgli.

Charles looks up, chastised. Tries to do both.

OVER ON THE STREET

Snakehead drives by again, nervously plotting his course.

BACK ON THE STAND

                    BRYAN
    Let me add, Mr. Darrow, one miracle is just as
    easy to believe as another.

                    DARROW
    Or just as easy not to believe.

                    BRYAN
    You have a definition of fact that excludes
    imagination.

DARROW

And you have one that excludes everything but imagination!

HICKS

I object to that as argumentative!

The crowd enjoys the confrontation. Neal and Malone smile.

The Prosecution team watches nervously.

In the crowd, Rappleyea, looks around. The Gangsters are gone. He keeps looking around for them. Sees the farm truck driving by.

JUDGE RAULSTON
(a little vengeful)
Colonel Bryan will get his chance.

DARROW

Mr. Bryan, do you believe Joshua made the sun stand still?

BRYAN

I suppose you mean, "Do I believe that Joshua made the earth stop revolving?"

DARROW

I am talking about what the Bible says. Did the man who wrote it think that the sun could be stopped?

BRYAN

I believe the man Joshua was inspired, and...

DARROW

Can you just answer my question?

BRYAN

When you let me finish the statement.

DARROW

It is a simple question, your Honor.

BRYAN
You cannot measure the length of my answer by the length of your question.

Laughter.

DARROW
No, except that the answer be longer.

More laughter.

BRYAN
I believe Joshua was inspired by the Almighty and that He used language that could be understood at that time rather than language that could not be understood until Clarence Darrow was born.

Laughter and applause. Charles laughs. It's a good point. But he stops when he sees Mencken giving him the evil eye.

DARROW
So, the language of the King James Bible is sometimes in need of interpretation, is it not?

BRYAN
Understanding, perhaps.

Neal and Malone wince. Another trap avoided.

DARROW
Fine. Now, Mr. Bryan, have you ever pondered what would naturally have happened to this planet if it had actually stood still?

BRYAN
God could have taken care of that, Mr. Darrow.

DARROW
Don't you know it would have been converted into a molten mass?

BRYAN
You may testify to that when you get on the stand.

Down in the press, Charles hides a smirk of appreciation from Mencken.

Darrow walks around, frustrated.

> DARROW
> Do you believe the story of Noah's flood to be literal?

> BRYAN
> Yes I do. A world-wide flood.

> DARROW
> When was that flood? About 4,000 years ago, according to the Bible?

> BRYAN
> I would not attempt to fix the date.

> DARROW
> What do you think?

> BRYAN
> I do not think about... things I don't think about.

> DARROW
> Do you think about things you do think about?

Laughter in the courtyard. But more wagging heads of scorn.

> HICKS
> Again, I object to the tone of this examination!

> BRYAN
> Let him have all the latitude he wants for I would like some latitude when he is on the stand.

> DARROW
> You can have latitude and longitude!

Laughter and some applause. Neal and Malone give each other a mischievous side-glance.

> DARROW
> You believe that every civilization on the earth was wiped out by Noah's flood?

BRYAN

Yes.

DARROW

Do you know a scientific man on the face of the earth that believes any such thing?

BRYAN

I cannot say.

DARROW

Are you even aware of how old civilizations are on the earth?

BRYAN

I have no great interest, Mr. Darrow, in those constant efforts by some to undermine the revelations of God Who was there --with the speculations of agnostics who were not.

There is prolonged clapping. Darrow is losing ground.

DARROW

I wish I could get a picture of this -- the bleacher seats.

BRYAN

Those whom you call "yokels"?

The crowd agrees with boos and hisses. Darrow rolls his eyes. The Judge pounds his gavel.

JUDGE RAULSTON

I will have none of this heckling in my court! Now, those in the audience shut up!

Hicks has had enough. He stands.

HICKS

Your Honor. This cross-examination has gone beyond the pale of any issue that could possibly be injected into this lawsuit!

> JUDGE RAULSTON
> To stop it now would not be fair to Mr. Bryan.

Hicks remains standing, his arms crossed. Bryan pumps a fan and pours himself a glass of water.

OVER ON THE STREET

Snakehead has parked his truck with a clear line of sight to the speakers' platform.

ON RAPPLEYEA

Rappleyea looks over and recognizes Snakehead with suspicion.

UP ON THE STAND

> DARROW
> Do you know about how many people there were on this earth 3,000 years ago?

> BRYAN
> Am I supposed to? You've called me as an expert on the Bible, not population statistics.

> DARROW
> No idea? No curiosity at all?

> BRYAN
> When you display my lack of knowledge, Mr. Darrow, could you give me the facts so I would not lack such knowledge any longer?

OVER BY THE PROSECUTION

Hicks to McKenzie:

> HICKS
> Darrow doesn't know the answers either.

UP BY THE STAND

> DARROW
> You'll get your chance, Mr. Bryan.

But Darrow's sly look to himself suggests otherwise.

>   DARROW
> You don't think much of scientists, do you, Mr.
> Bryan?

>   BRYAN
> Yes, sir, I do, sir.

>   DARROW
> Name one.

>   BRYAN
> George McReady Price. Professor of geology in
> Lincoln Nebraska.

>   DARROW
>   (with contempt)
> That small college?

>   BRYAN
> I didn't know you had to judge a man by the size
> of the college. I thought you judged him by the
> size of the man.

>   DARROW
> You mean by whether or not he agrees with your
> prejudice for the Bible.

>   BRYAN
> I don't think I am any more prejudiced for the
> Bible than you are against it, sir.

The crowd responds favorably. The Bailiff bangs his nightstick against the railing. They calm down.

And now a swirl of jump cuts of Darrow digging into Bryan, a swirling blur of chaos and skepticism...

>   DARROW
> Do you believe in the tower of Babel?

>   DARROW
> Do you know how many languages there are?

> DARROW
>
> Did you ever discover where Cain got his wife?
>
> DARROW
>
> Do you believe that there were dinosaurs inside Noah's ark?
>
> DARROW
>
> What about the religion of Confucius and Buddha?

IN THE CROWD

The heat bears down, spectators mop their heads.

Rappleyea is still watching Snakehead in the farm truck. Suddenly, he sees Snakehead fiddling with something. It's a rifle! Rappleyea's eyes go wide. He looks around frantically. Sees the Gangsters eating food, enjoying the trial in the shade.

UP ON THE STAND

> DARROW
>
> Mr. Bryan, do you think the earth was made in six days?
>
> BRYAN
> (he hesitates)
> Not six days of twenty-four hours.

OVER BY SNAKEHEAD'S TRUCK

Snakehead slips a bullet into the rifle's chamber. Cocks the rifle. Aims it at the stand.

SNAKEHEAD'S POV

Through the gun sight, focused on Bryan.

OVER BY RAPPLEYEA

Rappleyea is with the Gangsters. He points to Snakehead in the truck. The Gangsters see him.

> DARROW
>
> Not six days of twenty-four hours? Doesn't the Bible say so?

BRYAN
I do not think they were twenty-four-hour days. I think they were periods of time.

DARROW
Oh?

Mencken smiles and pokes Charles with his elbow. He looks up.

BRYAN
But I think it would be just as easy for God to make the earth in six days as in six years or in six hundred million years. Frankly, I do not think the question is important.

DARROW
Well, I do.

BRYAN
Your honor, they have not asked a question legally, and the only reason they have asked any question at all is to give this agnostic a stage upon which --

DARROW
Objection!

INTERCUT:

Between the argument on the stand and Snakehead trying to get a good shot in the truck, and the Gangsters and Rappleyea moving in on Snakehead. Rappleyea keeps getting in the way of the gun sight. As the pitch of the argument increases, the intended assassination draws to a climax...

BRYAN
(the volume rising)
I will answer his questions and I will answer them straightaway --because I want the world to see that this man...

DARROW
I object to that!

Bryan stands; two trains about to collide.

> BRYAN
> (louder still)
> ...is trying to use John Scopes and this trial to slander the Bible!

> DARROW
> (yelling)
> I am examining you on your fool ideas that no intelligent man on earth believes!!

There is a sudden silence except for the hollow echo of Darrow's words. Bryan sits. Darrow's hands shake, and he looks more the fool than his intended target.

BANG!!! The silence is shattered by a gun shot!

All heads turn. It's not a gun shot. It's a car back-firing.

OVER BY SNAKEHEAD'S TRUCK

The Gangsters have surrounded Snakehead and the Lead Gangster pulls him out of the truck, slams him to the ground. The Lead Gangster leans down into Snakehead's face.

> LEAD GANGSTER
> Time for a little justice. New York-style.

They pull him away.

BACK UP ON THE STAND

> JUDGE RAULSTON
> Court is adjourned!

There is a wave of noise, commotion, and movement toward the stage.

OVER BY SNAKEHEAD'S FARM TRUCK

Rappleyea draws near to the Lead Gangster.

> RAPPLEYEA
> I've got another opportunity for you gents.

The Lead Gangster looks at him curiously.

INT. AQUA HOTEL - DAY

Mencken and Charles walk briskly to Mencken's room. They turn a corner and almost plow into...

Rappleyea with the three big New York Gangsters behind him. Rappleyea is holding a newspaper. He shakes his head, disappointed, and reads.

> RAPPLEYEA
> "Bryan's oozing ignorance surprised even the foulest of the Tennessee swineherders, as he sought to keep his savages heated up, to lead his forlorn mob of imbeciles against the foe."

He drops the paper to his side with a disgusted sigh.

> RAPPLEYEA
> What's wrong with you Mr. Mencken? Why do you have to try and destroy Mr. Bryan and this town -- to make them into something that they're not? What are you so afraid of?

Mencken turns cold as a snake.

> MENCKEN
> Something that they're not? You mean like you? Pretending that you're a big-shot from New York City managing a world-class trial? When all you really are is a schmuck from Brooklyn trying to swindle real estate?

The Gangsters step closer, not appreciating Mencken's tone. But Mencken is right. Rappleyea regathers his confidence.

> RAPPLEYEA
> There's a three-thirty train out of Dayton, Mr. Mencken. You better be on it.

> CHARLES
> Rapp! He's just a reporter! You got no right to bully him...

                    RAPPLEYEA

          Who are you to talk about bullying, Charles
          Anderson? You're worse than Mencken -- bullyin'
          with words.
                    (gestures to Mencken)
          At least he didn't grow up with the people he
          mocks and lies about.

Charles is hit hard by this accusation.

Rappleyea turns.

                    RAPPLEYEA
          Let's go gentlemen.

But the Gangsters don't move. Rappleyea looks up into the Lead Gangster's eye. Gulps. You don't order this guy around.

But then the Lead Gangster nods and the four of them turn and walk away.

Mencken and Charles look at each other.

INT. MENCKEN'S HOTEL ROOM - DAY

Mencken packs his suitcase. A bit rushed, but also a bit energized by it all. Charles watches him.

                    MENCKEN
          You know what to write. Bryan's blistering
          buffoonery. Darrow's blinding brilliance.

He stops for dramatic effect.

                    MENCKEN
          Don't let me down, Mowgli. Make this a turning
          point in history. Go for the jugular.

Charles looks uneasy. Mencken finishes packing.

                    MENCKEN
          Speed is critical. This is your hour, kid. A good
          story now and you're in Baltimore by week's end.

CHARLES
(a holy whisper)
The Sun.

EXT. DAYTON MARKET STREET - DAY

Mencken and Charles race walk to the train station.

MENCKEN
Wire the news straight in, then get me a copy at the station by three-twenty nine. Don't be late!

CHARLES
What about the rest of the trial? You're going to miss the closing arguments!

MENCKEN
You still don't get it, do ya, kid? There aren't going to be any closing arguments.

Charles follows with a forlorn face.

EXT. RHEA COUNTY COURTHOUSE - DAY

Charles walks up the steps of the courthouse. Something strikes him and he pauses. Turns to look out on the city behind him. All the people. The families, laughing, playing. Simple folk, Townies. Without a care in the world beyond their small lives. Charles shakes his head with sadness.

INT. RHEA COUNTY COURTHOUSE - DAY

Charles stands alone in the quiet courthouse, looking around the room. He's haunted by the memories, the sights and the sounds of the past few weeks.

A black JANITOR cleans up in the corner. They lock eyes. The Janitor smiles and gets back to work.

INT. RHEA COUNTY COURTHOUSE - MOMENTS LATER

Charles, perspiring and alone in the courtroom, writes and writes. The pages turn in his note pad. The clock ticks.

EXT. COURTHOUSE LAWN - DAY

Now quickly crossing the Courthouse lawn on the way to the warehouse, Charles looks determined.

INT. PRESS WAREHOUSE STENO ROOM - DAY

Charles marches into the press warehouse steno room.

Rose is there at her machine. She sees him. Watches him walk right past her.

He pulls out his notes and sits in front of a different STENOGRAPHER. She peeks over at Rose who looks crushed.

Charles sees Rose too. He breathes a deep sigh and moves on.

> CHARLES
> I'm filing this with the Baltimore Sun.

EXT. TRAIN STATION MORNING

Mencken sits at an open window on the train. The engine idles and hisses. He breaks into a smile as Charles approaches. Charles, reaching up from the platform, hands him the story through the window.

> CHARLES
> Three minutes to spare.

Mencken looks at the paper. He reads for a few moments. His smile broadens. The train whistle blows.

> MENCKEN
> Mowgli, you sure can write.

> CHARLES
> Thank you, sir.

Mencken turns cold. Throws the papers out into the wind. They fly everywhere. Charles doesn't even flinch. He expected it.

> MENCKEN
> Of course, at the next train stop I'll kill that story with one phone call.

> CHARLES
> Yes, sir.

They stare at each other in silence. Respectful adversaries.

> MENCKEN
> So it turns out that you're like your father after all.

> CHARLES
> A great man once told me God's truth is never a losing cause.

> MENCKEN
> Well, good luck at the bottom of the food chain, Mowgli.

The train pulls from the tracks. Mencken pulls his head back in.

Charles watches the window fade into the distance. And suddenly he breaks down in tears, unsure of what he's just done. But holds himself. He's gonna stay strong.

He reaches into his shirt pocket and pulls out the cigar Mencken had given him for the day he "made it big." He lights the cigar, watching the train, he takes a puff and starts coughing.

Throws the cigar down and crushes it underneath his shoe.

He turns around, only to see Rose standing there.

> ROSE
> I read your article.

And for a moment, all time stops. And it's just Charles and Rose and nothing else in the whole wide world between them.

Charles can barely look at her.

She steps forward.

Charles opens his arms, pleading...

She runs into his embrace. They kiss like they've never kissed before in their lives.

He pulls apart from her. Looks at his watch like he's late again.

> CHARLES
> Abigail.

Rose has a look of newfound love for this man.

INT. SANITARIUM, ABBIE'S ROOM - DAY

Two Orderlies enter Abigail's room. She looks up with a smile.

>ORDERLY
>Hi, Abigail. Time for your surgery.

EXT. TENNESSEE ROADS - DAY

Charles's automobile peels down the road, dirt flying behind.

INT. SANITARIUM HALLWAY - DAY

A phonograph plays a scratchy record of some beautiful music of Wagner's softer moments. All for a calming effect on...

a slew of women tied down in bed carts along the hallway. Dr. Heydrich, dressed in operating gown and cap, and following another SURGEON walks up to Abigail's bed. The Surgeon's smock is full of blood spatterings. Abigail looks up scared at them.

>DR. HEYDRICH
>Hello, Abigail. This is Dr. Otto. He'll be taking care of you, today.

Abigail smiles weakly at the Surgeon.

>DR. OTTO
>Don't worry. Everything's going to be all right.
>We'll give you some ice cream afterwards.

EXT. SANITARIUM - DAY

Charles's car pulls up to the big sanitarium mansion.

INT. DR. HEYDRICH'S OFFICE - DAY

Dr. Heydrich begins pushing Abigail's bed cart down the hall. He smiles at her. A lifeless, dead smile. She's scared.

And suddenly the cart is stopped...

...by Charles and Rose blocking the way.

>CHARLES
>You're not doing this.

> ROSE
>
> I want my sister out of here.

> DR. HEYDRICH
>
> You signed the papers. This is illegal.
>> (yells down the hall)
>
> Security!!

Heydrich tromps up to them. Rose grabs the bed railing tight.

> ABIGAIL
>
> Rose, what's wrong?!

Heydrich tries to wrench Rose's hands from the rail. Charles helps Rose hold on.

> HEYDRICH
>
> Let go of my patient!

Finally, in frustration, Heydrich raises his hand to hit Rose. Freezes when he realizes what he's about to do. The Orderlies run around the corner. See it all.

> CHARLES
>
> If you don't let Abigail go, you'll be front page news until this place goes under or you lose your job. Or both!

Heydrich stares at Charles. Is it a bluff?

EXT. FRONT DOOR OF SANITARIUM - DAY

Charles, Rose and Abigail burst out of the doors with happy elation, carrying Abigail's suitcases. They bounce up to the car and pack it in. Rose stops Charles.

> ROSE
>
> Would you have really done that for Abigail? The front page?

Charles smiles lovingly at Abigail, who smiles back. Then he turns back to Rose.

> CHARLES
>
> Would have? Rose, I'm still gonna do it.

Rose grabs him and plants a big kiss on him. Abigail smiles with joy.

> ABIGAIL
>
> When do I get my ice cream?

INT. BRYAN RENTED RESIDENCE, DAYTON - NIGHT

Bryan is before the fireplace intent upon writing something. He stops, frustrated. Sighs. Mrs. Bryan is suddenly there in her wheelchair.

>				MRS. BRYAN
>	William.

He doesn't respond.

>				MRS. BRYAN
>	William, you don't have all the answers. Only God
>	does.

>				BRYAN
>	The papers are saying I looked like a
>	fundamentalist fool.

>				MRS. BRYAN
>	Only morons and imbeciles trust the newspapers.

That gets a slight smile from Bryan.

>				BRYAN
>	When I get my chance to examine Mr. Darrow
>	tomorrow, that'll even up things a bit.

>				MRS. BRYAN
>	Working on your closing arguments?

>				BRYAN
>	I've got to get it right. I've got to present our side
>	with real force.

>				MRS. BRYAN
>	What are you so afraid of, William?

>				BRYAN
>	I don't want to lose this case.

>				MRS. BRYAN
>	And you think that if you can only give your side
>	of the argument, you won't lose? You know as
>	well as I that people can hear all sides fair and

square and still choose the wrong because they're just too hog stubborn.

He nods. She's right about that -- too.

> MRS. BRYAN
> You're so afraid of losing your case and ending your career on a failure. Well, I got news for you, dear husband. Christ didn't get to present his side of the argument before Pilate.

That makes Bryan listen up.

> MRS. BRYAN
> And he lost his trial.

Bryan is getting it. He lights up with hope.

EXT. COURTHOUSE LAWN - DAY

The court is again assembled outside. A big day for all.

Charles sits with Rose, Abigail, and Mr. LeBarron.

> CHARLES
> Today Bryan puts Mr. Darrow on the stand.

> LEBARRON
> It's judgement day for Darrow.

Rappleyea is with the Gangsters.

Bryan is writing last minute changes on his notes.

Darrow stands before the Judge.

> DARROW
> Your Honor, we have no more witnesses to offer. I think to save time we will ask the Court to bring in the jury and instruct them to find the defendant guilty.

Surprise and rumbling in the crowd.

Bryan raises his eyebrows. Malone's head is down.

> JUDGE RAULSTON
> That is certainly an unprecedented request, Mr. Darrow.

The Prosecution team huddles. Talks to Bryan.

> HICKS
> That dirty scoundrel. He's sabotaging your chance to examine him. Cheating you of your closing argument!

> MCKENZIE
> The coward. He's running scared.

But Bryan pats them on the back. It's okay. He looks over at Darrow, who shoots him a snake-like grin.

But Bryan is not affected. Folds up his notes and puts them back into his suit coat.

> BRYAN
> It's okay, gentlemen. God doesn't need William Jennings Bryan to win his victories for him.

In Bryan's eyes is a peace. A realization of true victory.

EXT. RHEA COUNTY COURTHOUSE - DAY

The jury, returning in a solemn group, passes a spectator who looks at his watch.

> SPECTATOR
> Four minutes!

EXT. COURTHOUSE LAWN MORNING

Up on the platform, the Judge receives a slip of paper from the Bailiff. He glances at the paper, looks at the jury, and then looks up.

> JUDGE RAULSTON
> In the matter of the State of Tennessee vs. Thomas Scopes, the defendant, John T. Scopes, is guilty as charged.

The reaction of the crowd is restrained. No clapping, booing, or hissing. Just quiet murmurs.

The Judge's gavel hits.

INT. ROBINSON'S DRUGSTORE - DAY

Into the drugstore comes Rappleyea all excited.

> RAPPLEYEA
>
> Doc! Everybody! My 300 acres sold! Twice the price, and guess what? They donated the land to the city!

Everyone looks at him dumbfounded. They can't believe this from him.

Rappleyea rolls out a preliminary sketch of a college administrative building.

> RAPPLEYEA
>
> There's going to be a Bryan College! Our own college! Dayton is on the map for good!

EXT. TRAIN STATION PLATFORM EARLY AFTERNOON

At the Dayton train station, Darrow, Malone and Neal sit with their bags. Malone is reading the Christian Science Monitor.

> MALONE
>
> A pig.

> DARROW
>
> Who?

> MALONE
>
> A pig. Nebraska Man turns out to have been the tooth of an extinct pig.
> (laughs)
> Imagine that.

Neal shows him the paper. Darrow waves it away.

> DARROW
>
> Bah! Fundamentalist propaganda. Next thing you know, they'll be saying Piltdown man is a forgery.

INT. PRIVATE RESIDENCE USED BY BRYANS - DAY

A knock at the door. Bryan is there to open it.

It's Charles and Rose.

CHARLES
Mr. Bryan, I've come to ask your forgiveness.

BRYAN
For what?

CHARLES
I have written things about you in the papers - even about this town, where I've grown up - that I am not proud of.
(Rose hugs him)
Anyway, I know that you were robbed of your closing argument. And I know that speech is mainly what you came to our town to deliver.

BRYAN
God's providence, son.

CHARLES
Well, I would like to publish your closing argument, Mr. Bryan. I work at the newspaper in town. My father started it and he would be very pleased if what you wanted to say in Dayton could be published -- well, here in Dayton.

A big smile grows on the great Orator's face.

BRYAN
God's providence, indeed.

The three of them share a moment of intimate connection.

BRYAN
But I'm afraid, I'll have to ask you to leave.

Charles and Rose look at each other. Bryan smiles teasingly.

BRYAN
I was just about to lay my weary bones down and take my afternoon nap.

They share a laugh.

INT. BRYAN BEDROOM, MINUTES LATER - DAY

Bryan pulls his bed sheets back and gets in bed as he talks with Mrs. Bryan, in the background on her wheelchair in the kitchen, doing some knitting.

> MRS. BRYAN
> That young reporter from the local paper? What a
> fine young man.

> BRYAN
> You're right, dear.
> (more to himself)
> He's a fine young man.

And Bryan drifts off to sleep the sleep of the righteous.

EXT. DAYTON TRAIN STATION - DAY

We see an enormous crowd dressed in black around a funeral train in Dayton. At the back of the train we see a coffin draped in the American flag. Hicks and McKenzie are at the side of Mrs. Bryan. A band plays the hymn, "Faith of Our Fathers." Camera cranes up to reveal thousands of mourners lined along the tracks for a mile.

> CHARLES (V.O.)
> William Jennings Bryan died peacefully in his
> sleep in Dayton, Tennessee. Thousands came to
> pay their respects.

Out of the way of the big crowds, Clarence Darrow observes the ceremony with spite.

> CHARLES (V.O.)
> The ACLU sought to remove Clarence Darrow
> from the Scopes case on appeal because of his
> conduct in Dayton.

Judge Raulston, the Bailiff, Rappleyea, and others from the story are part of the sad crowd.

> CHARLES (V.O.)
> On that appeal, the Tennessee Supreme Court
> upheld the state statute as constitutional.

EXT. SCOPES HOME, DAYTON - NIGHT

Scopes throws sacks of unanswered mail onto a small bonfire.

> CHARLES (V.O.)
> John Scopes quit his teaching job in Dayton. He later admitted to never having taught evolution in the school room.

INT. DARK LIVING ROOM - NIGHT

A fireplace. Mencken in a wheelchair with a blanket on him. His face half drooped, motionless, he stares lifelessly into the flames.

> CHARLES (V.O.)
> H.L. Mencken suffered the last seven years of his life as a result of a stroke that left him unable to either write or speak.

EXT. THE SANITARIUM - DAY

A cold, dreary overcast day. The Sanitarium sits like an evil omen as Charles continues.

> CHARLES (V.O.)
> Over the next thirty years, 60,000 Americans would be involuntarily sterilized. Nazi Germany would model its eugenics program on American laws.

INT. DAYTON HERALD - DAY

Charles stands alone, looking sadly at his pamphlet press hard at work, printing.

> CHARLES (V.O.)
> As for Rose and me, after the eventful summer of 1925, I never asked her to marry me again.

Charles turns. Rose hands him a folio off the press. They kiss.

> ROSE (V.O.)
> Because I asked him.

She raises her hand to stroke his cheek. The wedding ring, big and bold on her finger. Charles sets the pamphlet down as they kiss...

The pamphlet is "CLOSING SUMMARY FOR THE SCOPES TRIAL BY WILLIAM JENNINGS BRYAN."

FADE TO BLACK:

"A fair result can be obtained only by fully stating and balancing the facts and arguments on both sides of each question."

-- Charles Darwin

THE END

If you liked this screenplay, check out the movie, *Alleged*, that was made from it:

On Amazon Prime here for purchase or rent.

More Screenplays as Literature

The Last Knight
An Historical Epic Movie Script About the Siege of Malta in 1565

Home Movies
A Family Comedy Movie Script About Time Travel and Family Dysfunction

Nietzsche: A Dangerous Life
An Historical Biography Movie Script About History's Most Infamous Atheist

John Brown's Body
An Historical Epic Movie Script About the Man Who Started the Civil War

Alleged
An Historical Drama Movie Script About the Infamous Scopes Monkey Trial

Death Before Dying
An Action Thriller Movie Script About a Hero Fighting Modern Day Pirates

Pressure Point
An Action Thriller Movie Script About Environmentalism and Corporate Murder

Descent of the Gods
A Horror Movie Script About a Reality TV Show and Alien Abduction

Double Life
A Psychological Noir Thriller Movie Script About Virtual Reality and Obsession

Noah Primeval: The Movie
An Epic Fantasy Movie Script About the Ancient World Before the Flood

A. D. 70
An Historical Epic Movie Script About the Fall of Ancient Jerusalem

Before I Wake
A Psychological Crime Thriller Movie Script About a Cop Who Can See Through the Eyes of a Killer

Cruel Logic
A Psychological Crime Thriller Movie Script About God's Existence and the Consequences of Ideas

To End All Wars
An Historical WWII Drama About Allied Soldiers in a Japanese Prison Camp

I receive commissions from links to Amazon books above.

Sign Up to Get Brian Godawa's Updates, Movie Reviews, Other Scripts & Books.

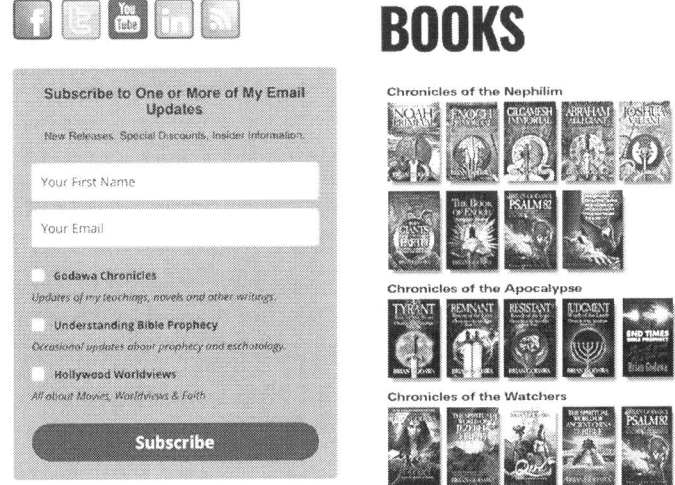

www.Godawa.com

Get 25% OFF the Informative Hollywood Worldviews Online Course

Limited Time Offer

How to Watch Films with Wisdom and Discernment
Amazing Video Lectures with Powerpoint and Film Clips!

Brian Godawa, Hollywood screenwriter and best-selling novelist, explores the power of storytelling in movies and in the Bible.

You will learn how storytelling incarnates meaning, worldview and redemption in movies.

You will discover the nature of subversion, and how narratives compete and win in the culture wars of both movies and the Bible.

You'll receive a Biblical foundation for understanding sex, violence and profanity in movies and storytelling.

And a whole lot more! Click the link below to see everything you will get.

The regular price is $139. You'll get 25% off if you use the coupon below. You'll pay just $104.25.

Use this Coupon Code to get 25% Off: SAL2525

https://godawa.com/hwc/

Book Series by Brian Godawa

See www.Godawa.com for more information on other books by Brian Godawa.

Chronicles of the Nephilim

Chronicles of the Nephilim is a saga that charts the rise and fall of the Nephilim giants of Genesis 6 and their place in the evil plans of the fallen angelic Sons of God called, "The Watchers." The story starts in the days of Enoch and continues on through the Bible until the arrival of the Messiah, Jesus. The prelude to Chronicles of the Apocalypse. ChroniclesOfTheNephilim.com (paid link)

Chronicles of the Watchers

Chronicles of the Watchers is a series that charts the influence of spiritual territorial powers over the course of human history. The kingdoms of man in service to the gods of the nations at war. Based on ancient historical and mythological research. ChroniclesOfTheWatchers.com (paid link)

Chronicles of the Apocalypse

Chronicles of the Apocalypse is an origin story of the most controversial book of the Bible: Revelation. An historical conspiracy thriller trilogy in first century Rome set against the backdrop of explosive spiritual warfare of Satan and his demonic Watchers.
ChroniclesOfTheApocalypse.com (paid link).

About the Author

Brian Godawa is the screenwriter for the award-winning feature film, To End All Wars, starring Kiefer Sutherland. It was awarded the Commander in Chief Medal of Service, Honor and Pride by the Veterans of Foreign Wars, won the first Heartland Film Festival by storm, and showcased the Cannes Film Festival Cinema for Peace.

He also co-wrote Alleged, starring Brian Dennehy as Clarence Darrow and Fred Thompson as William Jennings Bryan. He previously adapted to film the best-selling supernatural thriller novel The Visitation by author Frank Peretti for Ralph Winter (X-Men, Wolverine), and wrote and directed Wall of Separation, a PBS documentary, and Lines That Divide, a documentary on stem cell research.

Mr. Godawa's scripts have won multiple awards in respected screenplay competitions, and his articles on movies and philosophy have been published around the world. He has traveled around the United States teaching on movies, worldviews, and culture to colleges, churches and community groups.

His popular book, Hollywood Worldviews: Watching Films with Wisdom and Discernment (InterVarsity Press) is used as a textbook in schools around the country. His novel series, the saga Chronicles of the Nephilim is in the Top 10 of Biblical Fiction on Amazon and is an imaginative retelling of the primeval history of Genesis, the secret plan of the fallen Watchers, and the War of the Seed of the Serpent with the Seed of Eve. The sequel series, Chronicles of the Apocalypse tells the story of the Apostle John's book of Revelation, and Chronicles of the Watchers recounts true history through the Watcher paradigm.

Find out more about his other books, lecture tapes and dvds for sale at his website www.godawa.com.

BLANK PAGE

BLANK PAGE

BLANK PAGE

BLANK PAGE

Made in United States
Orlando, FL
07 July 2024